LANGUAGE AND LITERACY SERIES

Dorothy S. Strickland, FOUNDING EDITOR

Celia Genishi and Donna E. Alvermann, SERIES EDITORS

Writing Assessment and the Revolution in Digital Texts and Technologies
MICHAEL R. NEAL

Artifactual Literacies: Every Object Tells a Story
KATE PAHL & JENNIFER ROWSELL

Educating Emergent Bilinguals: Policies, Programs, and Practices for English Language Learners
OFELIA GARCÍA & JO ANNE KLEIFGEN

(Re)Imagining Content-Area Literacy Instruction
RONI JO DRAPER, ED.

Change Is Gonna Come: Transforming Literacy Education for African American Students
PATRICIA A. EDWARDS, GWENDOLYN THOMPSON MCMILLON, & JENNIFER D. TURNER

When Commas Meet Kryptonite: Classroom Lessons from the Comic Book Project
MICHAEL BITZ

Literacy Tools in the Classroom: Teaching Through Critical Inquiry, Grades 5–12
RICHARD BEACH, GERALD CAMPANO, BRIAN EDMISTON, & MELISSA BORGMANN

Harlem on Our Minds: Place, Race, and the Literacies of Urban Youth
VALERIE KINLOCH

Teaching the New Writing: Technology, Change, and Assessment in the 21st-Century Classroom
ANNE HERRINGTON, KEVIN HODGSON, & CHARLES MORAN, EDS.

Critical Encounters in High School English: Teaching Literary Theory to Adolescents, Second Edition
DEBORAH APPLEMAN

Children, Language, and Literacy: Diverse Learners in Diverse Times
CELIA GENISHI & ANNE HAAS DYSON

Children's Language: Connecting Reading, Writing, and Talk
JUDITH WELLS LINDFORS

The Administration and Supervision of Reading Programs, Fourth Edition
SHELLEY B. WEPNER & DOROTHY S. STRICKLAND, EDS.

"You Gotta BE the Book": Teaching Engaged and Reflective Reading with Adolescents, Second Edition
JEFFREY D. WILHELM

No Quick Fix: Rethinking Literacy Programs in America's Elementary Schools, The RTI Reissue
RICHARD L. ALLINGTON & SEAN A. WALMSLEY, EDS

Children's Literature and Learning: Literary Study Across the Curriculum
BARBARA A. LEHMAN

Storytime: Young Children's Literary Understanding in the Classroom
LARWRENCE R. SIPE

Effective Instruction for Struggling Readers, K–6
BARBARA M. TAYLOR & JAMES E. YSSELDYKE, EDS.

The Effective Literacy Coach: Using Inquiry to Support Teaching and Learning
ADRIAN RODGERS & EMILY M. RODGERS

Writing in Rhythm: Spoken Word Poetry in Urban Classrooms
MAISHA T. FISHER

Reading the Media: Media Literacy in High School English
RENEE HOBBS

teachingmedialiteracy.com: A Web-Linked Guide to Resources and Activities
RICHARD BEACH

What Was It Like? Teaching History and Culture Through Young Adult Literature
LINDA J. RICE

Once Upon a Fact: Helping Children Write Nonfiction
CAROL BRENNAN JENKINS & ALICE EARLE

Research on Composition: Multiple Perspectives on Two Decades of Change
PETER SMAGORINSKY, ED.

Critical Literacy/Critical Teaching: Tools for Preparing Responsive Literacy Teachers
CHERYL DOZIER, PETER JOHNSTON, & REBECCA ROGERS

The Vocabulary Book: Learning and Instruction
MICHAEL F. GRAVES

Building on Strength: Language and Literacy in Latino Families and Communities
ANA CELIA ZENTELLA, ED.

Powerful Magic: Learning from Children's Responses to Fantasy Literature
NINA MIKKELSEN

New Literacies in Action: Teaching and Learning in Multiple Media
WILLIAM KIST

Teaching English Today: Advocating Change in the Secondary Curriculum
BARRIE R.C. BARRELL, ROBERTA F. HAMMETT, JOHN S. MAYHER, & GORDON M. PRADL, EDS.

Bridging the Literacy Achievement Gap, 4–12
DOROTHY S. STRICKLAND & DONNA E. ALVERMANN, EDS.

Crossing the Digital Divide: Race, Writing, and Technology in the Classroom
BARBARA MONROE

Out of This World: Why Literature Matters to Girls
HOLLY VIRGINIA BLACKFORD

Critical Passages: Teaching the Transition to College Composition
KRISTIN DOMBEK & SCOTT HERNDON

(Continued)

Making Race Visible: Literary Research for Cultural Understanding
STUART GREENE & DAWN ABT-PERKINS, EDS.

The Child as Critic: Developing Literacy Through Literature, K–8, Fourth Edition
GLENNA SLOAN

Room for Talk: Teaching and Learning in a Multilingual Kindergarten
REBEKAH FASSLER

Give Them Poetry! A Guide for Sharing Poetry with Children K–8
GLENNA SLOAN

The Brothers and Sisters Learn to Write: Popular Literacies in Childhood and School Cultures
ANNE HAAS DYSON

"Just Playing the Part": Engaging Adolescents in Drama and Literacy
CHRISTOPHER WORTHMAN

The Testing Trap: How State Writing Assessments Control Learning
GEORGE HILLOCKS, JR.

School's Out! Bridging Out-of-School Literacies with Classroom Practice
GLYNDA HULL & KATHERINE SCHULTZ, EDS.

Reading Lives: Working-Class Children and Literacy Learning
DEBORAH HICKS

Inquiry Into Meaning: An Investigation of Learning to Read, Revised Edition
EDWARD CHITTENDEN & TERRY SALINGER,
WITH ANNE M. BUSSIS

"Why Don't They Learn English?" Separating Fact from Fallacy in the U.S. Language Debate
LUCY TSE

Conversational Borderlands
BETSY RYMES

Inquiry-Based English Instruction
RICHARD BEACH & JAMIE MYERS

The Best for Our Children
MARÍA DE LA LUZ REYES & JOHN J. HALCÓN, EDS.

Language Crossings
KAREN L. OGULNICK, ED.

What Counts as Literacy?
MARGARET GALLEGO & SANDRA HOLLINGSWORTH, EDS.

Beginning Reading and Writing
DOROTHY S. STRICKLAND & LESLEY M. MORROW, EDS.

Reading for Meaning
BARBARA M. TAYLOR, MICHAEL F. GRAVES,
& PAUL VAN DEN BROEK, EDS.

Young Adult Literature and the New Literary Theories
ANNA O. SOTER

Literacy Matters
ROBERT P. YAGELSKI

Children's Inquiry
JUDITH WELLS LINDFORS

Close to Home
JUAN C. GUERRA

On the Brink
SUSAN HYNDS

Life at the Margins
JULIET MERRIFIELD, ET AL.

Literacy for Life
HANNA ARLENE FINGERET & CASSANDRA DRENNON

The Book Club Connection
SUSAN I. MCMAHON & TAFFY E. RAPHAEL, EDS., WITH
VIRGINIA J. GOATLEY & LAURA S. PARDO

Until We Are Strong Together
CAROLINE E. HELLER

Restructuring Schools for Linguistic Diversity
OFELIA B. MIRAMONTES, ADEL NADEAU, &
NANCY L. COMMINS

Writing Superheroes
ANNE HAAS DYSON

Opening Dialogue
MARTIN NYSTRAND, ET AL.

Just Girls
MARGARET J. FINDERS

The First R
MICHAEL F. GRAVES, PAUL VAN DEN BROEK, &
BARBARA M. TAYLOR, EDS.

Envisioning Literature
JUDITH A. LANGER

Teaching Writing as Reflective Practice
GEORGE HILLOCKS, JR.

Talking Their Way into Science
KAREN GALLAS

The Languages of Learning
KAREN GALLAS

Partners in Learning
CAROL LYONS, GAY SU PINNELL, &
DIANE DEFORD

Social Worlds of Children Learning to Write in an Urban Primary School
ANNE HAAS DYSON

Inside/Outside
MARILYN COCHRAN-SMITH & SUSAN L. LYTLE

Whole Language Plus
COURTNEY B. CAZDEN

Learning to Read
G. BRIAN THOMPSON & TOM NICHOLSON, EDS.

Engaged Reading
JOHN T. GUTHRIE & DONNA E. ALVERMANN

Writing Assessment and the Revolution in Digital Texts and Technologies

Michael R. Neal

FOREWORD BY **JANET SWENSON**

Teachers College, Columbia University
New York and London

Published by Teachers College Press, 1234 Amsterdam Avenue, New York, NY 10027'

Library of Congress Cataloging-in-Publication Data

Neal, Michael R.
    Writing assessment and the revolution in digital texts and technologies / Michael R. Neal ; foreword Janet Swenson.
        p.   cm. — (Language and literacy series)
    Includes bibliographical references and index.
    ISBN 978-0-8077-5140-4 (pbk : alk. paper) — ISBN 978-0-8077-5141-1 (cloth : alk. paper)
    1. Educational technology.   2. Language and languages—Study and teaching—Technological innovations.   3. Web-based instruction.   I. Title.

    LB1028.3.N44 2011
    428'.00285—dc22

                                                                                2010031488

ISBN 978-0-8077-5140-4 (paper)
ISBN 978-0-8077-5141-1 (hardcover)

Printed on acid-free paper
Manufactured in the United States of America

18   17   16   15   14   13   12   11   8   7   6   5   4   3   2   1

For Matt and John

Contents

Foreword by Janet Swenson   *ix*
Acknowledgments   *xi*

Introduction: Writing Assessment as and with Technology   1

PART I: WRITING ASSESSMENTS AS TECHNOLOGIES

1. Underlying Assumptions of Writing Assessments
    as Technologies   15

    Instrumentalism and Its Resultant Neutrality   *18*
    Determinism and Its Resultant Invisibility   *23*
    The Transparency of Writing Assessments as Technologies   *27*
    Moving Beyond Instrumentalism and Determinism   *31*

2. Cultural Narratives That Characterize Writing Assessments
    as Technologies   33

    Technotopic Narratives of Writing Assessments as Technologies *34*
    Technophobia: Pessimistic Narratives of Technology   *37*
    Toward a More Balanced Approach to Technology   *41*

3. Decision Making and Development of New Assessment
    Technologies   42

    Implementation   *44*
    Prediction   *46*
    Design   *53*
    Finding a Place at the Table   *55*

PART II: WRITING ASSESSMENTS WITH TECHNOLOGIES

4. The Mechanization of Writing Assessments with Technologies   59
    *The Propensity of Writing Assessment to Move Toward
    Mechanization*   *60*

    The Path to Machine-Scored Student Writing   65
    Writing Experts' Experiences with Machine-Scored Writing   70
    The Misdirection of Mechanization   74

5. Hyperactive Hypertechs   76
    Hypertext: Connectivity Articulated   78
    Hypermedia   91
    Hyperattention   99
    Becoming Hypersensitive   104

6. Assessing the Texts and Techs of the Digital Revolution   106
    Construct Validity as a Means of Assessing Hypertechs   109
    Writing Outcomes as a Means of Assessing Hypertechs   120
    Old Frameworks for New Assessments   126

Conclusion: The (R)evolution of Writing and Its Assessment   128

Bibliography   135
Index   145
About the Author   153

Foreword

RECENTLY, I BEGAN physical therapy for joint pain. Both my doctor and the therapist explained that my physical response to stress had resulted in a misalignment of my body, making everyday tasks painful. Much the same can be said about the impact of assessment on many writing programs and curricula in both K–12 and postsecondary settings. The stress of external pressures on the assessment of student compositions, writing programs, and educational institutions has, in far too many cases, resulted in a painful misalignment of our work as educators.

In his provocative book *Writing Assessment and the Digital Revolution in Texts and Technologies*, Michael Neal notes that teaching writing and assessing writing are inextricably linked to each other. Teaching involves understanding our students' current capacities, intervening in some meaningful way, and determining the effect of the intervention, realizing that some effects may not become apparent for weeks, months, or even years, and other desired effects don't manifest themselves in response to assessment algorithms. He reminds us of what others (Dewey, Freire, hooks, Giroux, and Delpit, to name just a few) have pointed out before him: Teaching is a political act. Therefore, assessment, an integral component of teaching, is also never neutral, but instead informed by our understanding of the purpose of schooling and education, the roles of teachers and students, the selection of materials and methods, and the contexts in which education occurs.

In his text, Neal artfully weaves together narratives, definitions, histories, and practices that are related to writing, assessment, technology, and teaching. He observes that new forms of composing (blogs, wikis, documentaries, podcasts, etc.) that emerging technologies make more readily available to us and to our students, have created an exigency for us. We find ourselves in need of answers to these two questions: How will we assess these new compositions? What will we sacrifice, if anything, in stretching or re-imagining the writing curriculum to weave in these new communicative forms and opportunities?

Neal then seems to echo White House Chief of Staff Rahm Emanual's observation, "You never want a serious crisis to go to waste . . . it is an opportunity to do things that you [thought] you could not do before."

Neal argues, convincingly, I believe, that the time is precipitous, not only to consider how we will assess new forms of composition able to be developed for new audiences and purposes in new contexts, but also to make productive use of this "crisis," to consider more holistically the role assessment has and should play in our teaching and our students' learning, and how best to realize the beneficial role we imagine for assessment.

As we read, we are asked to differentiate our thinking about assessment as a technology that helps us think more critically and productively about our and our students' aspirations for writing and assessment that is more distant from the classroom, less often intended to improve instruction and more often reflective of binary, positivist and reductive conceptions of student learning. It is this latter approach to assessment that worries Neal as he leads us from a consideration of assessment *as* a technology to assessment *with* technology. In tracing cultural understandings of technologies as generally positive, beneficial, efficient, and economical, he demands that we, if we haven't already, become engaged in making assessment technologies visible and demanding that they themselves be critically assessed.

Of particular concern to Neal is the lure of "economy," a characteristic often associated with any technology and most often understood in our cultural narratives to be universally beneficial. Neal worries aloud that unless we productively trouble the relationship between the economy of responding to student writing and authentically beneficial methods of responding to student writing, we leave ourselves open to machine scoring of student essays, an assessment method that is touted for its capacity to attain what to Neal are misguided understandings of validity and reliability. Whether we see promise or peril in such methods of assessment, Neal exhorts us to reclaim control of when, where, how, and most important, why our students are assessed.

Wisely, Neal tempers these calls with an acknowledgement of the complexities of teaching contexts that are highly variable and that hamper the ability of many writing teachers to wrest control of assessment from those whose primary intent appears to be something other than enabling individual students to grow as writers. One of these intents, Neal observes, may be to marginalize or silence those who work most closely with students, and who may wish to draw the broader public's attention to a wide array of social problems that inevitably influence what happens within classrooms. Although aware of the constraints that many writing teachers negotiate daily, Neal's call to action reminds me of Diane Ravitch's admonition to us: "The greatest obstacle to those who hope to reform American education is complacency."

—Janet Swenson

Acknowledgments

I HEARD AN ELOQUENT address several years ago that began with the speaker's acknowledging that anything valuable in the forthcoming speech should be attributed to the wisdom and generosity of her mentors and that any shortcomings were hers alone. I share that sentiment as I complete this book. That a person could have such wonderful mentors and colleagues might be something we all hope for, but few have been as fortunate as I have been in this respect.

I was introduced to writing assessment by Brian Huot during my doctoral work at the University of Louisville. I came into the program with an interest in technology as it related to social justice, and under his guidance, I learned how writing assessment was a productive outlet for those interests. He taught me not only assessment theory, but also what assessments look like on the ground when they worked to promote the interests of teaching and learning. He also showed me through his example how to direct and assess a writing program in ways that valued student learning and teachers' professionalism.

I have also been the beneficiary of generous mentoring from Kathleen Blake Yancey, who despite responsibilities in the field too numerous to mention, took the time to show me how to put my interests to good use through faculty development workshops, work with secondary teachers, and consulting with writing programs and organizations across the country. She has seemingly boundless energy, which she channels into the very best causes within the discipline and into the well-being of students and teachers. I have seen her interact with people at conferences and on campuses who have been helped and encouraged by her knowledge, enthusiasm, and support. I write this as one of those fortunate people.

I have also had many wonderful colleagues and students to work with over the course of writing this book. Whether they know it or not, many of them have been sounding boards for these ideas and provided me with valuable feedback. Of special note is my colleague Kristie Fleckenstein, who is as good a responder as she is a writer. Especially at the formative stages of this project, she read proposals and abstracts and offered insights that shaped the framework of the book. I also want to acknowledge the support of my home institution, Florida State University, in their support of this project.

Even more so I would like to acknowledge the support of my family. My wife, Christy, and my children, Isaac, Hallie, and Alec, simultaneously give me reason to do the work I do and keep me grounded in things of greater value. As in any endeavor that takes this amount of time, my family has been supportive of the extra hours that I have put into this project.

Writing Assessment as and with Technology

Civilization advances by extending the number of important operations which we can perform without thinking of them.
—Alfred North Whitehead

THE ESSAY Christine composed for my class was in many ways like others I have received in my years of teaching. Hers was a particularly smart argument about the vital role of satire in political commentary and critique. Using the media frenzy around the cover image of Barack and Michelle Obama on the November 21, 2008, *New Yorker* as evidence, Christine suggested that political humor can be an effective means to communicate complex ideas to an informed, savvy audience. Despite the widespread media outcry against this image, showing the couple dressed in Islamic and militant attire and giving each other the now-famous "fist bump," Christine claimed that this image was only one in a long line of edgy, political statements made by *New Yorker* covers that poked fun more at American ignorance and stereotyping than at anything negative about the people depicted.

While it is not uncommon for an image to be of central importance in an essay—various writing and language courses at the secondary and postsecondary levels have long engaged with visual media, popular culture, and cultural critique—Christine's essay is unique, in that it is a multimodal composition. She composed a 6-minute digital video essay that included a narrated audio script accompanied by video news footage from Fox News, CNN, and MSNBC; still photos of political analysts, *New Yorker* covers and cartoons, and candid moments of laughter from otherwise serious political figures; a secondary audio music track that ran under the narration; and a short video excerpt from a *Seinfeld* episode in which Jerry, Elaine, and George puzzle over the obfuscated meaning of a *New Yorker* cartoon. Christine's multimodal essay—an example of what Cynthia Selfe (2004) calls "new media" because it is a text "created primarily in digital environments, composed in multiple media (e.g., film, video, audio, among others), and designed for presentation and exchange in digital venues" (p. 43)—was created in an otherwise traditional English class, not one that was earmarked for experimental genres of writing. It was both my privilege and responsibility to assess the assignment. Although I assigned this type of hybrid, multimodal text and encouraged Christine to produce it, little in my formal education or subsequent professional development had prepared me for such an assessment moment: to respond to it, to evaluate it, or to grade it within the larger context and outcomes of a writing course.

As I travel virtually and physically across the spaces of English classes and look at the teaching of writing at both the secondary and college levels, I find that Christine is not so rare in composing in new media, nor am I alone as a teacher faced with assessing new-media texts. Although I believe that new-media texts are less common in secondary education largely because of the overwhelming burden of teaching to standardized tests, students at every level of education compose in a variety of media outside class. Students are not only producing writing in digital forms; they are also including original or found images, digital video, audio narration, and music. Further, they are composing texts in digital environments (e.g., blogs, wikis, digital videos, podcasts, social networking sites, and a variety of Web 2.0 applications) that tap into their capacities to think and communicate in multiple modalities that rely on an expanding and diverse range of 21st-century literacies.

Much of the current discussion surrounding new literacies revolves around teachers' keeping up with the latest technologies our students are using and discovering how we can use them to accomplish goals within our writing classes (Ball & Kalmbach, 2010; Colby & Colby, 2008; Devoss & Porter, 2006; Vie 2008). Or we are engaging in increasingly difficult questions of copyright and plagiarism of digital texts that now include visuals, audio, and design as well as traditional print texts (Johnson-Eilola & Selber, 2007; Howard, 2007; Rife, 2007) and network infrastructures (DeVoss, Cushman, and Grabill, 2005). We know that new-media texts are informed by complex rhetorical situations and thus we are invested in the discussion. And we know that texts include more than just the printed word, even though that is where many of us have resided professionally for most of our careers. Most would acknowledge that texts and technologies are evolving faster than our teaching of writing, though many of us can point to individuals who have developed inventive digital writing assignments. Systemically, though, we are still trying to figure out where new-media writing fits within the framework of our curricula. It may be fine when individual teachers and students experiment with new technologies, but what might this look like on the broader scale, and is this even a direction we want to move toward as a field? What would we have to give up in order to include it, and what would be lost?

Most of us in the field, I would suggest, live with a type of tension in which we remain unfamiliar or uncomfortable with many of the new technologies, and yet we do not want to be resistant to healthy evolution or become obsolete in light of the rapidly changing landscape of English instruction. While institutional and individual technological capabilities are increasing and new-media literacies resonate with many teachers, as of yet we do not have a clear vision of why (or even if) these new literacies are worth pursuing outside the sense that students engage in composition that taps into their tacit knowledge and literacies from their out-of-school experiences. Most of us who have experimented with multimodal composing have witnessed a level of student engagement—not across the board, but with a great number of students—that indicates their eagerness to move in this direction. However, it is reasonable to question whether student engagement alone is enough to justify reshaping writing curriculum to include new-media composition and if there aren't other ways to connect with students that don't require such an investment in time and resources. It is also reasonable to question what this shift to digital writing will cost us in unintended side effects.

Writing assessment provides us with one framework that responds to these concerns because it offers a systematic structure to engage questions about student learning and the outcomes associated with writing curricula. Through assessment at the individual, classroom, and programmatic levels, we might be able to determine ways that new-media texts work toward our expressed goals and objectives and ways they do not. Writing assessments can include anything from large-scale assessments (e.g., program assessment, placements, standardized testing) to responding to, grading, or otherwise evaluating individual student texts (e.g., portfolios, graded essays, and responses of all types). One of the problems we encounter with writing assessment is that it can become something too specific for many of us, depending on our position in relationship to it. Therefore, we often miss each other's point, because for one of us writing assessment is bound up with standardized testing, while for another it is grading student essays, and yet for another it means programmatic assessment. While all these are legitimate sites for writing assessment, it is important to understand the multifaceted nature of writing assessments that exist outside our own personal connections with it.

Writing assessment can also inform student outcomes and course goals, which may need to evolve in response to changes in digital texts and technologies. I believe that such change is the cause of much of the anxiety over new media. Such an initiative would require us to revisit the outcomes and goals to determine which are essential and central to our mission as opposed to those that are tangential or further dilute the vision of writing instruction, a concern often expressed by those who are resistant to new-media writing. It is one thing if digital technologies clearly embrace and enhance existing outcomes and goals, but it is a different dynamic if the technologies challenge or undercut them. Even though I tend toward embracing digital media, I validate that concern. While my teaching experience revolves around college writing courses, my work with secondary English language arts teachers indicates that it is equally worrisome across educational contexts. Courses with direct writing instruction—especially 1st-year college composition—cannot be everything to everyone, nor can they include everything that might justifiably fit within their scope and vision. Our time with students is precious, their needs are great, and those of us who teach writing cannot continue to add more to the curriculum without considering what it will replace. This tension forces us to make important value judgments every time we teach. So for me the question is not whether instruction and assessment of new-media texts—or other uses of digital technologies—is justifiable in the classroom, but whether it is the best use of our limited resources in helping students achieve desired outcomes.

In the interest of full disclosure, though, I should reveal some of my own biases and assumptions. While I am sympathetic to the concerns about the ways digital technologies may be changing the way we write and assess writing, my record teaching college writing, administrating writing programs, and working with secondary language arts teachers demonstrate that the way I think about writing, communicate about writing, teach writing, and assess writing are all consistently informed by emerging technologies.

Digital technologies are embedded within the fabric of many composition outcomes and state writing standards that steer instruction and assessment of student writing. In my home state of Florida, the Sunshine State Standards affirm that a student "selects and uses a variety of electronic media, such as the Internet, information services, and desktop publishing software programs, to create, revise, retrieve, and verify information" (9–12 Grade Language Arts, LA.B.2.4.4). Even though I tend toward interpreting technology into my own teaching and research, in many instances in the chapters that lie ahead I take a decidedly negative stance toward certain applications of writing and assessment technologies. I consider myself neither antitechnology nor protechnology. As I write this I realize that my not staking out a claim in one familiar camp or the other might adversely affect my ethos with many readers. I do not consider technologies the problem or the solution, and if we approach them either way, we reinforce an unhealthy divide.

My purpose in this book is to illuminate several points of intersection between writing assessment and technology to show how the cultural expectations of technologies shape our expectations of writing assessment. The technological path we are currently going down with writing assessment is in many ways contrary to the rhetoric nature of writing, which causes it to become a site for frustration and resentment among many teachers. However, this is not the only technological path available to writing assessment. So rather than taking an antitechnology/assessment stance, I suggest several high-tech directions we can go in with writing assessment that are consistent with the outcomes and directions we want to pursue as educators. In my examining writing assessment and technologies in tandem, though, a two-pronged complication arises for students and educators, because by their very nature, assessments are technologies; however, writing assessments also increasingly involve digital technologies.

To show the difference between these two uses of technology, I make a distinction between writing assessments *as* technology and writing assessments *with* technology. Because all writing assessments are technologies—from high-tech applications such as ePortfolios and computer scored writing to low-tech iterations such as the in-class handwritten essay and the written response—they inform many of the habits and notions we have developed in contemporary educational settings. The most detrimental effect of such assumptions is that educators have become (often unintentionally or against our better judgment) proponents of writing assessments that often are reductive and at odds with our best understanding of teaching and learning. But we have done this under enormous external pressure and a technologically driven management system that strips teachers of their ability to make decisions based on the best interests of their students.

With the increasing viability and visibility of digital texts and technologies, we are in what I believe is a finite, kairotic juncture with writing assessment. We have this opportunity, while the texts and technologies are relatively new, to reframe our approaches to writing assessment so that they promote a rich and robust understanding of language and literacy. If we do not, we will follow the path to assessment technologies that was mapped out in the 20th century, in which assessment largely promoted reductive views of language in favor of the modernist agenda of efficiency, mechanization, and cost effectiveness. As is often the case when promoting a radical shift—a revolution of sorts—we have real obstacles.

But it is an effort that is worthy of our pursuit because the consequences are high for us and, more important, for our students. Understanding writing assessment *as* and *with* technology provides a framework that can help us promote a transformation that can lead us and our students into practices that reflect and respond to the ways technologies and texts are evolving in the digital age.

PART I: WRITING ASSESSMENTS *AS* TECHNOLOGIES

Too often the writing assessments we use to make decisions about students and programs do not adequately account for writing as engaged, rhetorical literacy events that occur within complex social contexts and relationships. What we know about effective writing and assessment is often eclipsed by concerns of evaluating ever-increasing populations of students with diverse writing needs and abilities in highly politicized academic environments of ever-dwindling financial and personnel resources. I am not surprised that under the enormous demand to assess student writing quickly, efficiently, and cheaply, education has largely bought into the promises of technological solutions. Either that, or educators have abdicated our responsibility to speak with resolve in the face of top-down educational structures that silence those who would otherwise advocate for better practices.

The promises of technological fixes to social and educational problems are particularly plausible because they tap into deep-seated assumptions that are woven into the fabric of our cultural consciousness (Volti, 2001). Several crucial assumptions and narratives of technology influence the ways in which we understand writing assessments, which in turn inform why certain assessments hold such powerful sway over educational practices and are difficult to dislodge even when better models and ideas are presented. Although the cultural narratives of technology may vary, several dominant attitudes toward it appear indelibly etched into our collective cultural consciousness that in turn affect the ways we understand writing assessment to function.

Ron Westrum (1991) likens the cultural tendencies toward certain views of technology to undertow: "In the ferment of social and technological change, it is often impossible for us to see the direction in which we are going, or to understand the trends in which we participate. Like swimmers caught up in a powerful undertow, we are swept along into new experiences and new innovations" (p. 4). Extending Westrum's metaphor, ocean swimmers must learn how to respond when caught in a powerful undertow that threatens to take them away from their intended destination. Instead of expending valuable energy swimming against the undertow (and ultimately becoming exhausted in the process while all the while being swept further out to sea), the swimmer is far more likely to reach the safety of the shoreline if she swims perpendicular to the water's force until she finds a path of less resistance and then angles in toward her goal. Some writing assessments can be likened to swimming directly toward the goal but ultimately not making much, if any, progress.

Without our being conscious of the powerful forces that influence cultural understandings of technology, it is unlikely that we will be effective in promoting writing assessment reform that will last beyond the significant outpouring of individual energies and resources in specific localities. Yet even these local efforts are worth noting because they help us identify the destination and show us what writing assessments can be. While it may not be most judicious to swim directly against the forces of cultural assumptions, neither can we stop resisting and merely "go with the flow," since we have become increasingly aware of where the undertow is dragging us. I will note only briefly here the federal No Child Left Behind initiative, the state-monitored educational standards, and the Spellings Commission. These are not viable options, nor are they moving us in a direction in which we want to go, and yet they are exactly where the cultural assumptions about assessment as technology are leading us. We would be better stewards of our limited resources and energy if we moved perpendicular to the powerful cultural assumptions of technologies, exploring the potential of digital technologies and identifying places of less resistance where we can progress toward defined goals that will provide multiple stakeholders with the necessary information to make informed and responsible decisions about students, teachers, programs, and institutions.

Writing assessments are one clear occurrence of educational technologies (Huot, 1996a, 2002; Madaus, 1993, 1994; Takayoshi, 1996). Madaus (1993, 1994) established a case for this connection in the early 1990s, showing how values that underlie many assessments—such as utilitarianism, economic competition, technological optimism, objectivity, bureaucratic control and accountability, numerical precision, efficiency, standardization, and conformity—are parallel to the values often associated in Western society with technology. He further asserts that all assessment technologies share a similar structure:

> All types of evaluation rest on the same basic technology. That is, we elicit a small sample of behavior from a larger domain of interest—for example, algebra or general aptitude—to make inferences about a person's probable performance *relative* to the domain. Then, on the basis of these inferences,

we classify, describe, or make decisions about individuals or institutions. (1994, p. 77)

The basic assessment technology relies on gathering information and using that data to make educational decisions, about either people or institutions. Our attitudes toward technologies in general affect our understanding of a more specific technology—writing assessment—that in turn shapes the ways that we often imagine it to function within varying educational contexts.

In viewing all writing assessments as technologies, we can see not only how they are designed to function but also the often unintended consequences that accompany their implementation. In most cases, though, new assessment technologies are touted for their promise and potential. Educators, corporations, and nonprofits develop writing assessments with the idealistic hope that the new technology will be generally beneficial for students and allow stakeholders to make important decisions based on their results. Even though I believe that some organizations are less responsible and ethical than others, I assume that very few people in educational assessment go to work each morning desiring to tyrannize students and undercut teachers that particular day. Yet we are beginning to understand more clearly the types and extent of the damage being done in the name of writing assessment and upholding standards.

It would be unwise, though, to vilify writing assessment or its developers. I know how it feels to introduce myself as an assessment person, and believe me, it's neither a crowd pleaser nor a way to establish a good first impression. But education could not exist without assessment, and when done well, writing assessment can be central to facilitating the best teaching and learning environments possible. In any case, writing assessments directly influence teaching and learning as they take place in classrooms, in programs, in schools and their systems, in states, across the country, and around the world. Donald MacKenzie and Joy Wajcman (1985) claim that technologies are constitutive of society; in other words, they are not a separate entity that exists and interacts within society, but rather are what makes society possible in the first place (p. 23). In the same way, writing assessments are constitutive of writing instruction.

Understanding the ways in which technology assumptions and narratives function in relationship to writing assessment explains where we are, how we got here, and most important how we can promote healthy evolution so writing assessments can be as productive as possible in the digital age. Since the assumptions and narratives tend toward hyperbolic extremes that are neither accurate nor helpful, we need to find alternative ways to describe writing technologies and assessment that are likely to resonate with disciplinary experts as well as writers in and out of the classroom.

Educators with experience and expertise in writing should assume more responsibility in developing new writing assessment technologies, especially since we are in the position to provide an informed vision of the direction writing is heading into the 21st century. If we wait until implementation to critique and then attempt to resist the new application, it will often be too late to exert meaningful influence. We will remain in the roles that we now largely occupy—conscientious objectors or reluctant accomplices—rather than being productive advocates for better writing assessments if we cannot look forward to where writing and its assessment are going and do not get involved earlier in the process. Because we have largely relegated the role of developer and designer of assessments to technology experts, their visions, limitations, values, and needs consistently trump those of teaching and learning that are more central to our discipline.

PART II: WRITING ASSESSMENT WITH TECHNOLOGIES

The second section of the book shifts from an examination of all writing assessment as educational technologies to a closer look at digitized writing assessment, in terms of both high-tech technologies for assessing writing as well as our assessment of high-tech texts. A closer look at writing assessments with technology reveals how the assumptions and narratives explored previously play out in the digital age. While some high-tech applications align with the assumptions and narratives that have dominated writing assessment for decades, others are poised to promote writing as a variable, rich, and complex rhetorical activity. Inasmuch as writing assessments with technology allow for more local, rhetorical decision making and analysis, they also become capable of responding to the increasingly sophisticated new-media texts that writers are composing in and out of the classroom.

The mechanization of assessment practices and procedures is one of the dominant tendencies that have carried forward from print to digital technologies. Bolstered by the widespread acceptance that technologies promote speed, reliability, and efficiency, mechanized writing assessments continue to proliferate and make claims that often miss the point of writing assessment in the first place. Often, writing assessment is so ubiquitous in educational settings that we see it as an end in itself rather than a means to communicate something meaningful to students, teachers, or institutions. If assessment is understood as the ultimate goal, it makes sense why we would value things like speed, reliability, and efficiency over learning. Those aren't necessarily bad values until they compromise the meaningful information that assessments are supposed to gather, or until they result in negative educational consequences that impose inequities.

Machine-scored writing, the most obvious form of mechanized digital writing assessment, promises to relieve overburdened teachers of the "mundane" work of reading, responding to, and grading student writing while at the same time threatening to replace human teachers and challenging the very notion of what it means to read and write. While machines cannot read in the traditional sense, they count in exponentially more sophisticated ways that enable them to score student writing with highly reliable results (Jones, E., 2006; Wohlpart, Lindsey, & Rademacher, 2008). When students write for machines rather than for human audiences, the rhetorical situation and an author's position dramatically shift, damaging a nuanced and sophisticated notion of writing that has been central to writing instruction for decades.

While machine scoring might be the most blatant application of writing assessments with digital technologies, other, more subtle applications have led us to the place where we are now, including some that have been widely implemented in recent years: grading rubrics, holistic scoring, and assessment-driven electronic portfolio systems. While each local application of such instruments is not equally mechanistic, those that value data mining, surveillance, and centralized control of decision making function at the expense of teacher expertise and student agency in the writing process. While companies profit from selling costly new assessment technologies (and many educators have bought into the culture of data mining or the fear surrounding academic integrity in the digital age), it is not in the best interest of students, teachers, or the discipline to adopt assessments such as these, even though they are marketed as a high-tech solution to educational problems.

Mechanization is not the only tendency, though, with digital writing assessments. Writers in and out of the classroom are producing more digital texts in response to increased access to and proliferation of online composing technologies that I believe are poised to work against the more reductive forces of mechanized writing assessment. At least three characteristics of digital composition have affected contemporary writing and its assessments: hypertexts, hypermedia, and hyperattention. In response to the connectivity allowed and encouraged by hypertext, portfolios—this time of the electronic variety—have reemerged in classrooms, schools, programs, and institutions in ways that resemble their initial popularity during their heyday in the 1980s–1990s. In addition to the connections writers can demonstrate via ePortfolios, writing assessment in the 21st century needs to respond to the ever expanding notions of composing and writing in the digital age. Sometimes referred to as *new media* or *multimodal composition*, hypermedia texts draw from a variety of media and modalities, presenting writers with unique rhetorical choices that result in new opportunities and challenges for writing assessment that we will explore in this section. Finally, hyperattention—defined by N. Katherine Hayles (2007) as "characterized by switching focus rapidly between different tasks, preferring multiple information streams, seeking a high level of stimulation, and having a low tolerance for boredom" (p. 187)—differs from both hypertext and hypermedia, since it is not a textual characteristic but rather a characteristic of the writer and perhaps the reader, and yet the ramification for writing assessments are clear. Historically, educators have valued student writing that is characterized by focused deep attention. This is one of the primary ways in which the technologies might be driving a change in student-writing outcomes in our classes, though it is not clear how we as a discipline should respond to it.

In response to the changing nature of writing and assessment technologies, the book concludes with practical principles, guidelines, and suggestions for assessing writing in an age of digital texts and technologies. In terms of a large-scale assessment of student writing, students' texts can be assessed fairly and appropriately without an excessive emphasis on mechanization, which has been the hallmark of large-scale assessment practices for decades. Large-scale writing assessments should value human response, the communication of useful information, connections to the local curriculum, and local teacher expertise—all characteristics that have been demonstrated to be feasible but work against the dominant assumptions and narratives of educational assessment.

Shifting to classroom assessment, three common approaches have emerged in response to teachers faced with the challenge of assessing new-media texts: (1) treating them the same as print texts, (2) importing criteria and language from other disciplines, and (3) developing assessment rubrics or scoring guides. Building on work from such notables as Cheryl Ball (2004, 2006), Ellen Cushman (2004), Jeff Rice (2003), Cynthia Selfe (2004), Jennifer Sheppard (2009), and Craig Stroupe (2007), I argue that part of a writer's work in the 21st century is to determine the appropriate content and modes to most effectively communicate with his or her audience, and the work of the evaluator continues to be providing robust, engaged feedback and evaluation that acknowledges the rhetorical sophistication of digital texts and technologies.

The problem remains of finding ways to determine which digital-writing assessments are worth pursuing and which are best left behind.

It is counterproductive to think that we can effectively incorporate every new digital text and technology in our teaching and assessment of writing. The sheer volume of options available to us is overwhelming and growing daily, which puts most of us as teachers in unfamiliar and uncomfortable territory. Even the most tech savvy among us have probably had some experience thinking that either we can't keep up or we can't squeeze one more thing into an already packed curriculum. While I lay out arguments for and against specific applications, the ever evolving world of technological development suggests that by the time this print book reaches its audience, a new set of high-tech applications will be emerging. Therefore, my goal is to focus less on the specific applications and more on the ways we consider the relationship between digital texts and technologies for writing assessment that we can apply as they continue to emerge and evolve.

Inasmuch as writing assessment technologies enable students and instructors to attain authentic writing contexts for teaching and learning, we should encourage their use. However, many writing assessment technologies are aligned with a different set of values that work against a situated, rhetorical approach to writing and result in educational inequities that have plagued assessments in the past century. Despite the need for change, the most influential assessment models today are bolstered by their strong connections to prevailing cultural assumptions and narratives of technology that result in technologies that endorse good writing as on-the-spot production of texts with few surface errors, a formulaic arrangement without reading or social interaction, and a diminished rhetorical sophistication. These assessments allow us to manage and compare mass populations of students and reduce the educational "burden" of writing assessments, but they fall short of helping students develop as writers and of promoting healthy students, classes, and curricula. In part because of the influence of writing assessment technologies, the writing that students produce in college classes is too often inauthentic, radically different from what we know to be the best practices in the teaching and assessment of writing. This troubling mismatch between what we know about writing and its assessment is further complicated by the continually rising influence of digital technologies in the writing classroom and in writing assessment.

PART I

Writing Assessments as Technologies

Underlying Assumptions of Writing Assessments as Technologies

We live in a society exquisitely dependent on science and technology, in which hardly anyone knows anything about science and technology.

—Carl Sagan

TECHNOLOGIES PROFOUNDLY INTERSECT social institutions such as education in such a way that it is nearly impossible to study or understand one without considering their mutual relationship. Since some of the earliest technologies—from tools that aided in the gathering and preparation of food to weapons of war and hunting—people have been fascinated by them and have pursued newer and better alternatives. Langdon Winner (2004), whose work in technological sociology has been influential for decades, suggests that perhaps the most prevalent view of technology is that it will largely improve or benefit society (p. 34). It is not surprising, then, that educators, politicians, students, and administrators most often understand new writing assessments as having the promise to accomplish everything from solving the latest literacy crisis to relieving educators of the time-consuming "drudgery" of reading and responding to student writing. This view of technology seems daunted neither by the audacity of its promises nor by the inability of previous technologies to live up to their expectations. While in some ways the history of technology can be told by a list of "successful" inventions, another equally accurate representation might be a list of unfulfilled promises and expectations. The assumption of progress positions writing assessments in such a way as to solidify their current status while simultaneously perpetuating the need for new developments that espouse new hope when the current models inevitably don't meet expectations.

In addition to the fanfare of progress, technological change paradoxically functions as a source of anxiety and pressure for many. Nearly everyone has experienced such tension, whether it be difficulty adjusting to Microsoft's latest operating system, frustration over a nearly obsolete computer that was purchased only months earlier, unfamiliarity with the latest social networking application, or shame about the limited capabilities of our cell phones. We are developing a collective "tech envy" that forces comparisons to what others have and that engenders an underlying fear of becoming outdated, even among the most faithful technology users and early adopters. Although we as teachers of English and writing may be gaining in technological sophistication, it may come at a great cost. Deborah Brandt (2001) identifies the "unending cycles of competition and change [that] keep raising the stakes for literacy achievement" (p. 2), and the same may be said of technological literacies. As quickly as we figure out ways to effectively teach writing with a new technology, others become available that separate those on the cutting edge from the rest, creating a multitiered hierarchy. It seems as though we as teachers are constantly in pursuit of the latest teaching technologies—including those for writing and its assessment—and yet the learning curve is accelerating far faster than we could ever hope to keep up with, and the expectations for what students can and should do is escalating out of reach as well for many of our students.

As technological changes raise expectations, opportunities, and challenges for writers, it also creates a type of instability that students and teachers must negotiate. While the dominant cultural position of technology remains one of optimism and progress, it necessarily coexists with tensions. Writing teachers are not exempt from the obligation of responding wisely and appropriately to technological change. A central disciplinary concern has been and will continue to be how to respond to the shifting landscape of writing technologies. Most of us desire to respond to the changing nature of digital texts and technologies, though we may be uncertain about how to proceed and if we have the time and resources to develop a sustainable model for investigating and integrating new technologies. We wonder how applications such as social networking, digital video, podcasts, wikis, blogs, and other new-media technologies can or should be assimilated into our classes and what we could possibly give up to make room for them. We wonder if our vision for writing has grown too far afield from the print texts that have been central to our teaching for years. We wonder if we should be developing new courses for these new texts and technologies.

If we believe that digital texts and technologies should be an integral part of the curriculum, we wonder if we have the expertise to teach them to an ever expanding and diverse population of students. We wonder if we have the infrastructure that will support them at our institutions. We wonder if they will help or hinder our students in becoming better writers, thinkers, rhetoricians, researchers, workers, and citizens. In short, we have pressing questions about digital texts and technologies that we are only beginning to answer, and we are likely to have more questions as the technologies proliferate and look less and less like traditional print literacies.

Instead of looking at these dilemmas primarily in an attempt to make sense of the newest and least established forms of digital texts and technologies, we establish a framework for responding to them by looking at how all writing assessments are and have been technologies and, as such, function in ways that are relatively predictable. Dennis Baron (1999) reminds us in "From Pencils to Pixels: The Stages of Literacy Technologies" that while most discussions of technology connote a type of high-tech aura, even low-tech composing options, such as pen and paper, are just as much a technology (p. 18). The same would be true of writing assessments as technologies. A holistic scoring session of print texts is just as much an assessment technology as computer-scored writing. If we can identify some major patterns in the ways we have responded to older writing assessment technologies, we might be able to respond with better judgment and critical distance to newer technologies with that framework as a guide. Baron expands on that premise in *A Better Pencil: Readers, Writers, and the Digital Revolution* (2009) by noting that each new writing technology expands the notion of who can be an author (p. 11). Likewise, many of the latest technological developments in writing assessments seem to widen their scope. As politicians turn to assessment technologies for educational accountability through systemwide state-mandated assessment, the appeal of many new assessment products is their ability to blanket an entire population of students to determine if any are being left behind.

With an eye toward the ways in which writing assessments as technology—both as material objects and as abstract knowledge and procedures—have been developed and implemented in educational settings, this chapter explores two key cultural assumptions about technologies and the resultant effects that influence ways in which writing assessments are often framed: (1) instrumentalism that leads to technological neutrality and (2) determinism that leads to invisibility. The purpose of this framework is less about addressing, supporting, or critiquing specific assessment technologies and more about identifying larger cultural trends and ways of thinking about technologies that influence our understanding of and response to writing assessments. They are two identifiable and often competing attitudes about technology in general that exert influence on our perception of more situated technologies such as writing assessments. If we can identify how writing assessments as technologies have been positioned by these dominant cultural assumptions, we are in a position to better

1. recognize our current, vexed relationship with many writing assessment technologies,
2. understand why certain writing assessments or their marketing strategies have been more successful than others,
3. analyze the current choices we have to make regarding the assessment of digital texts and technologies, and
4. develop a sustainable plan for determining which digital texts and technologies to integrate into the writing curriculum of the 21st century as well as how to assess them.

INSTRUMENTALISM AND ITS RESULTANT NEUTRALITY

Central to any definition of technologies is that they are things people use or create to accomplish a specified purpose (Green, 2002; Haas, 1996; Huot, 1996a; Madaus, 1994). This general definition directs our focus on the materiality of technologies, *things* people use to accomplish tasks. Emphasizing the physical nature of technologies, Christina Haas (1996) notes that they are "materially embodied symbolic tools that humans use for the goal-directed accomplishment of work—work that is communicative, economic, or intellectual, or, more likely, work that is all of these at once" (p. 6). While rocks might not be a technology, since they are natural objects, they become one when people use them for a purpose, such as to pound a stake into the ground, to form a wall for protection, to divide property, or to keep domesticated animals in a particular area. However, technologies are more than mere physical objects; they are also processes, procedures, or techniques. In other words, the technique involved in building a solid rock wall is as much a technology as the material objects used in the process. We tend to think of writing assessment technologies as the test (e.g., essay test prompt, SAT multiple-choice questions, or the scantron); however, more abstract procedures or knowledge such as holistic scoring, writing outcomes, grading policies, response strategies, or portfolio scoring guidelines are as much a part of the assessment technology as are the physical apparatuses.

Even though technologies are purposeful or made to address issues or problems, we also must acknowledge that they often function beyond and in unintended ways. One way to consider how technologies function within a society is to look at the purposes or needs that initiate their construction as well as the unintended consequences of their adoption. For example, the exigency for an assessment might be to identify students who need additional time, support, and assistance to successfully complete programmatic writing outcomes. This is a laudable goal. Just as important, though often overlooked, is the need to examine a fuller range of social and educational consequences that result from the assessment technology. What we might not have expected, though, from the previous example are "side effects" such as the financial burden or educational stigma of noncredit courses for which students pay or a secondary writing curriculum that might advocate a "back to the basics" mentality toward developmental writers.

The problem with an instrumental view of technology is that technologies are far more common than the latest digital devices, and an exclusive focus on the physical equipment conceals their complex ideological qualities, the processes by which the technologies function, and the wide-ranging social consequences of their production and use. It also ignores nonmaterial technologies such as systems, processes, and techniques. While writing assessments are composed in part of their physical apparatus, they do not accurately represent the full extent to which writing assessments are technologies. Within this instrumental framework, the goal for educators and assessment companies is too often the development and implementation of the ideal testing instrument, which they see as one that has the ability to function for a number of purposes, decisions, and contexts rather than one that focuses on the local needs of a student population or a single decision. Test developers deem the ideal testing instrument as one on which "right answers" can be scored reliably so to minimize error and thus make the instrument objective and fair. By focusing exclusively on the instrument, we often ignore deeper underlying assumptions about writing assessment such as what "right answers" might look like on a writing test, the decisions that are being made based on the results of the test, or the negative social consequences perpetuated by many assessment systems. When our focus is on the test or the instrument, it is easy to ignore or miss the larger technological system at work within writing assessments.

Enormous financial and human resources are wasted in the attempt to develop and refine assessment instruments for multiple purposes and contexts without considering the full range of the technological system, including the procedures, processes, and consequences of the decisions that will be made based on their results. Instead of considering the fuller context of writing assessments, we seem to prefer tweaking flawed assessment systems as if we could correct their problems by somehow refining them. In this way the "problem" with most assessments is incorrectly identified as having yet to develop the right instrument to produce reliable results rather than as looking at how and why decisions are made based on the results gathered by the assessment.

While large testing companies are easy—but fair—targets, the acontextual mass marketing of writing assessments or the focus on testing instruments happen at more local levels within our programs and schools. Highly influential scholars in writing assessment often propose the same writing assessment instrument or method across contexts and student populations as if the solution were in the instrument itself rather than the way it is used and implemented to make decisions about local students, teachers, or programs. We should be wary of assessment experts who "sell" their pet solutions rather than investigate local needs and student populations. Likewise, presentations and workshops often advocate for a type of uncritical adoption of an assessment across contexts, disregarding particular places, purposes, and contexts. Many educators comb conferences, looking for instruments such as the ideal rubric, ePortfolio platform, or placement procedures, as if a one-page handout or Web site were the answer to their assessment needs. While we can and should learn from existing writing assessment systems, we cannot assume that the answers to our problems can be addressed by developing and mass marketing instruments regardless of context.

The educational, social, and economic contexts that surround the use of a writing assessment are also important considerations in the overall structure. Take, for example, an impromptu essay test for student placement into 1st-year writing in which there are countless considerations and elements of which the technology is composed. The essay prompt as well as the pen-and-paper composing situation are parts of the overall technology; so are the underlying motives of the administrators for determining this use of timed writing tests, creating the test questions, and scoring the essays. If the essays are scored holistically, there are a multitude of factors that compose that technology, including the readers, the scoring guide, the calibration or norming session, benchmark essays, and the trait descriptors, to name just a few. The strategies students use to compose their essays are all part of the technological system as well as the courses into which they may be placed and their curricula. Even in a non-traditional placement assessment such as directed self-placement (DSP), a rich context surrounds students' deciding which class best suits their needs and interests that might include such elements as a survey instrument, academic advising, the courses into which they can be placed, the explanation of those courses, and the differing reasons students have for selecting one course over another—the list could go on. The point being, technologies are much more complete and complicated when the people, objects, motives, and uses are all considered as part of the overall technology. An instrument is only one small portion of the overall picture of the technology.

When technologies are viewed primarily as instruments or tools, the tendency will be to ignore their larger social and educational contexts.

When writing assessments are understood as instruments, we think of them as neutral tools, objects, methods, or procedures that people use in order to make a decision or make the process easier, faster, or more efficient or to meet some other desirable end. Neutrality has been consistently identified by scholars over a number of years as a danger in the way we relate to technologies (Haas, 1996; Heidegger, 1977; Selfe; 1999). A technology on its own or before it is used is likely to be understood as value free. Langdon Winner demonstrates how instruments—or artifacts, as he calls them—are anything but neutral, with the example of how approximately 200 bridges in Long Island surrounding Jones Beach, a highly acclaimed public park, were purposefully constructed with a 9-foot clearance in order to prevent public buses from reaching the park (1985, pp. 29–30). The technological instrument—in this case the bridges surrounding the park—were ideological even before they were built and used because of their design and political motivation.

A series of events that occurred when I was the director of 1st-year composition at a midsize state university illustrate this principle to me. The situation started with a seemingly innocuous event: a student-organized raffle. This type of fund-raising happens frequently on college campuses nationwide. However, in this case the stakes were raised, since the artifact being raffled was an AK-47, which by state law could be owned and operated by anyone over the age of 18 who was not a convicted felon. The logic, stated so concisely it can fit on a bumper sticker, is that guns are inanimate objects that cannot in and of themselves do any harm, which makes them value free: "Guns don't kill people; people kill people." Thus, the law only speaks to the kind of person (felon or nonfelon) who can be in legal possession of the gun. The appeal of this logic is its simplicity. If accepted at face value, however, it leads to specific political action as well as social consequences. In this case it might appear more reasonable to pass laws about gun use rather than about gun manufacturing, marketing, or ownership, since their use will largely determine their value.

The timing of the gun raffle coincidentally overlapped with an assignment in 1st-year composition to engage in writing as social action. Many of the composition instructors in the program at that time allowed their students to determine the specific topic for their project. Not surprisingly because of the visibility and controversy surrounding the raffle, several students and classes chose to write against the raffle, regardless of their political orientation. In fact I was initially surprised by how many students who were passionately against the raffle began by self-identifying as conservatives. Because the attention became so focused on the political agendas of the parties involved in the controversy, few people thought to challenge the initial premise of the argument, namely, the neutrality of the AK-47.

Several students and teachers, though, did their homework, and they made the argument that instruments are ideological, and the AK-47 was so in particular ways because of its history, function, and capacity. In other words, context matters. An instrument that might be one thing in the jungles of Vietnam might be something very different in a student apartment complex. The fallacy that these students avoided was twofold: (1) simply reassigning the instrument with a different ideological position so that instead of it being necessarily good, it becomes necessarily bad, and (2) in assuming that because context matters, the instrument would be neutral or value free. These logical traps are easy to fall into, especially when we have a worthy agenda to promote, and yet seeing this play out in a few external examples might help us turn a more critical gaze toward writing assessments as instrumental technologies.

If bridges and guns cannot be neutral but are rather ideological, regardless of the ways people use them, writing assessments are not so different a technology as we might imagine. Take, for example, the defense of the written portion of the SAT verbal test presented by the College Board and Educational Testing Service (ETS): institutions decide if, how, and when to use the results from the assessment for whatever educational decisions they want (e.g., admissions, 1st-year composition placement/exemption, ESL testing). The tacit assumption is that the test instrument is essentially neutral or value free until educators use their results, relieving the test developers and promoters of any responsibility for it. They argue for the objectivity of the test and the statistical reliability of its scoring, but they do not feel compelled to defend larger assumptions behind the assessment system. For them it's a major move to actually look at student writing, and for them that's enough. They don't, for example, critically examine the conditions where they collected the writing sample, the environments in which writers compose, the lack of an authentic context or audience for the writing, or the way the writing sample is combined with their traditional standardized testing model to determine the students' verbal scores. As in the case of bridges and guns, standardized assessment can at first seem appropriate and fair.

However, standardized test development includes a norming process by which questions are eliminated based on how certain groups of students score (Garcia & Peason, 1994). The problem occurs because if minority students, who are most often underrepresented in the sample, do well on questions upon which majority students do poorly, questions are still likely to be eliminated (p. 343). No matter the original intent of the assessment or its current uses, standardized tests that are normed to majority populations of students—whether that is defined by race, gender, income level, or other demographic factors—students who are underrepresented in the sample population are disadvantaged in the process (Darling-Hammond, 1994; Garcia & Pearson, 1994; Madaus, 1994; Mercer, 1989).

Now that we know that the standardized tests such as the SAT predictably results in racial and gendered discrimination in higher education, how should we respond? It is insufficient for ETS to tweak the instrument to make it better. Furthermore, we cannot look for a new instrument to replace the old one as if the broken one could be replaced by one that works. No instrument—even ones that I believe can be helpful in achieving beneficial ends (e.g., ePortfolios, directed self-placement, reflection, dynamic criteria mapping)—can stand alone as a solution. Rather, we need to consider the entire writing assessment system, including the accuracy and appropriateness of decisions we make based on it, to find more valid ways of assessing student writing within local contexts and individual needs.

It is not our goal to find an assessment instrument that is neutral and fair. Instead, we need to develop and implement writing assessment technologies that reflect values consistent with teaching and learning that have been the foundation of our discipline and that work in specific contexts for specific purposes. To do that we need to consider the full context surrounding the assessment, including the student populations; the content of our curricula; the decisions we make based on the results of assessment instruments; and just as important, the social and educational consequences that result from those decisions.

DETERMINISM AND ITS RESULTANT INVISIBILITY

In many ways a foil to instrumentalism and its resulting neutrality, technological determinism—the belief that the technologies themselves shape and define the culture, largely independent of human interaction—results in a type of technology invisibility and most often positions people as passive victims, while the technology itself is the active agent (Westrum, 1991, p. 15). From this perspective, technologies often appear to support or promote their own growth and development so that, in essence, they exert agency over their own prospects. Sherry Turkle (2004) suggests that one of the predominant concerns behind what she calls "the spin" on contemporary technologies is an anxiety about the "soul of the machine and the mechanization of the mind" (p. 26). While this description might initially conjure up pop culture images of Terminator- or Cylon-like cyborgs turning against their human makers or Matrix-like systems in which machines enslave human populations for their own exponential growth, determinism has less sci-fi expressions as well.

Recently when I was online with Firefox, an error occurred, but instead of the more typical message I expected, what I received started like this, "Well, this is embarrassing…" My initial response was to chuckle at the cleverness of this approach. It was a strangely effective human-like response. Instead of feeling frustration that the program failed, I was inclined to be more "forgiving" and give it another chance. As I think about this more, though, I am increasingly seeing examples of how we human-ize our technologies. Online searches like Ask Jeeves attempt to provide a more personal interaction with the machine. Many people name their cars or computers or other technologies, talk to them, and personify their actions. By humanizing our technologies, we create the illusion that they are more personal and relational than they are. Even though this might be effective marketing, it is important to distinguish between human and machine interaction. Once those lines become blurred, the rhetorical situation gets clouded as well.

In addition to the humanization of technologies, Turkle points out that people are becoming mechanized in this system. Students in our classes are learning to write in increasingly mechanistic ways in order to score well on assessments. Nearly 2 decades ago I was teaching a dual-enrollment writing class to a group of high school seniors, who were busily completing their state-mandated portfolio at the same time. While I was instructing them in nuanced rhetorical principles to apply to their writing, they were simultaneously engaged in a distinctly arhetorical writing situation. At one point in the semester the students were passing around a list of words they were all supposed to include in the cover letter of their portfolio, since their teachers had determined that cover letters with those words scored higher than others. I suppose one might argue that this is a type of audience analysis, but it was turning the student from the role of author into that of a thoughtless scribe. It did not matter how the words were used, what their meanings were, or what the writers hoped to communicate to the audience. It only mattered that certain impressive vocabulary words made it on the page. I am concerned that the types of writing assessments we use are mechanizing the minds of students in ways that are contrary to what we are or should be teaching them about writing.

Inevitability, which is a vital component of technological determinism, is also present in a related concept often referred to as the *technological imperative*. The technological imperative has at least two common usages: (1) much like determinism, it suggests that because technologies are inevitable, they should simply be accepted, but it also means that (2) because technologies are available, they should be used or implemented. The former is often used in predictable ways, namely, to argue that resisting new technologies is futile and that people are better off simply accepting changes without resistance, since they are unavoidable. The latter has an important difference. This use of the imperative goes beyond mere intellectual acceptance of a technology to its implementation and use: "The imperative implies that the invention of a new technique *demands its adoption and development,* and although there are countless examples of 'useless' inventions that no one wants and which are not developed but fade away, the general tendency has been to pursue possible developments for their own sake" (Shallis, 1984, p. 64; emphasis mine). The addition of active adoption raises the stakes for the individual in relationship to an assessment. It is one thing, for example, to acknowledge that composition is changing and includes digital technologies and multimodality, but it is a high level of commitment to change assignments, modify courses outcomes, or develop new courses in digital texts.

This push toward implementation can play out in writing assessment in different ways. For example, once something like a COMPASS test or an SAT verbal exam exists, some are bound to suggest that because they are available, they should be used indiscriminately. Their existence is reason enough to adopt them and make important educational decisions based on them. It is much harder to resist a technology that is readily available. For example, when I administrated a 1st-year writing program, the institution decided to purchase a site license for a popular plagiarism-detection program. Once it was accessible and effectively marketed to the decision makers in the institution (not the faculty, in this case), it became more difficult to talk and think about the technology in critical ways. While individual faculty members could choose not to use it in their classes, it was an ever present entity: Students knew it could be used at any time, and faculty did not have the power to remove it from the course management system in which it was embedded. The technological imperative worked in at least two ways in this case: (1) the software's existence, along with an aggressive marketing scheme, suggested to institutional decision makers that the "problem of plagiarism" could be framed in such a way that the new technology would "solve" it, and (2) the inclusion of the software in the course management system suggested to faculty and students that it was an effective and ethical countermeasure to detect and deter student cheating.

Most technologies have become so much a part of our lives that we often interact with them without considering the political, social, and otherwise ideological implications of their development, uses, or consequences (Haas, 1996). On a typical morning, I don't give a second thought to my digital alarm clock that wakes me to an lousy impersonation of wind chimes, the gas water heater and the plumbing that pumps hot water to my shower, the straight-edge razor and fogless mirror I use to shave, the soap with which I wash to clean myself, or the shampoo and conditioner I use to conceal my thinning hair. In fact, I only give them any thought when they are conspicuous in their absence or failure. If my alarm clock doesn't go off, I'll oversleep and my kids will be late to school. If the hot water heater is on the blink, I'm quick to notice the discomfort of a cold shower in which I'll inevitably cut myself shaving in the fogless mirror that ironically has been permanently hazy since its 1st week of use. And heaven forbid if I run out of my hydrating soap or have to use a different shampoo and conditioner that will cause me to suffer the indignity of dry skin and bad hair all day. Even in these contexts, however, where I pay attention to technologies that are normally invisible to me, I still don't think of them as technologies or think of them beyond the inconvenience of their not being present or working properly. Each of these technologies doubtless has a long history of and context for its development, production, and use. Unless a person makes a concerted effort to investigate such matters, the context and history of the technologies we use quickly fades into obscurity.

The older and more ubiquitous the technology, the less likely we are to notice or spend any time thinking about it. That is why it's important for us to examine newer digital writing and writing assessment technologies now, while they are still relatively new and thus visible. Already many of the ways we write and assess writing in the digital age are becoming transparent to most educators and students alike. Most of us have experienced the inconvenience of being without an important writing, networking, or communication technology for a certain time (e.g., Internet down when we are supposed to send or receive an important e-mail, iPhone out of range at the weekend retreat in the mountains, course management system down the day students are supposed to turn in their final projects into the digital drop box). Do we as teachers and writing experts move beyond the frustration of failed technology to a more critical examination of those technologies, or does this become equivalent to one of our "bad hair" days? Can we even see the technologies for how they shape us and our thinking about writing and communicating?

A few years ago my laptop crashed at a time that I had to be away from my home and office computers but had to produce 10 to 12 pages of finished text over the weekend. This technological failure provided me with fascinating insights into my own writing habits with digital technologies that had become transparent over years of access. My first reaction to the new-old technology was physical: My hand hurt as I wrote. I don't mean some slight ache that I could push to the back of my mind; I mean severe cramping that was so painful I was forced to focus on it rather than what I was writing. I had to consciously think about not gripping the pen so hard and force myself to keep my pen moving on the page. Second, I noticed how slowly I wrote longhand as compared to my keyboarding skills that I've always considered lackluster at best. The speed, or lack thereof, of my writing slowed my pace to the extent that I had a difficult time staying focused on what I was attempting to communicate. In fact, I found my mind wandering, since it was bored waiting for my hand to catch up with the thought. It wasn't all negative, though. I found that emotionally I was connecting with my writing in a fresh way and that I felt a sense of accomplishment with the physical flipping of the pages rather than the endless scrolling of the word processed document. I also remember having a renewed sense of my document's structure and flipped back through the pages far more frequently than I do with a word processor, where I have more trouble finding previously written sections and fear losing my spot when scanning through the document. While I drafted the document by hand and did some editing and proofing manually, I waited until I had a digital document before I did any larger revisions and editing, the primary focus of composition scholars' early research on the effects of word processing on writers (Bean, 1983; Bridwell, Nancarrow, & Rosscite, 1984; Collier, 1983; Harris, 1985, Sudol, 1985). Overall, though, the experience was eye opening for me because I was able to move beyond the inconvenience of writing by hand to a more critical examination of how reliant I am on word processing and how it has fundamentally changed many of my writing habits in ways that I had not noticed.

I believe that a similar phenomenon has occurred with writing assessments and will continue to occur without our even noticing them unless we challenge the underlying assumptions of how they function as technologies. Most of us do not even think about the mandated portfolios anymore or the SAT questions or the timed, impromptu essay beyond figuring out ways to score highly on them. Too many teachers and students have come to accept them uncritically and have not had enough experiences with alternatives to examine the common assessment technologies more critically.

THE TRANSPARENCY OF WRITING ASSESSMENTS AS TECHNOLOGIES

Whether the assumption is instrumentalism leading to neutrality or determinism leading to invisibility, both lead to a dangerous place: the transparency of writing assessments as technologies. Writing assessments can become transparent for a number of reasons, but three are of particular interest in light of the assumptions outlined previously: (1) transparency caused by commonality, (2) transparency caused by widespread institutional acceptance, and (3) transparency caused by more pressing concerns within a particular assessment context. As computer-assisted learning and writing environments are becoming more commonplace, many of the technologies associated with digital composing run the risk of becoming invisible by their ubiquitous presence in our lives. While some composition teachers remember the advent and development of word processing technologies, others do not and students even less so. To them, word processing as well as blogging, instant messaging, texting, and posting may be so much a part of their daily practices that they have no critical distance from which to reflect on the ways their practices in those spaces shape the way they compose and understand their literacy practices. They are what Marc Prensky (2001) calls "digital natives," people who have grown up with digital composing technologies that are perfectly natural for them and are relatively unaware of their influence. Without thinking about composing technologies as such, their influence—including ways that shape authorship, writing processes, distribution of texts, and so on—again lurk under the surface ignored, even though they have significant implications for literacy and the teaching of writing.

Other writing technologies have followed the same pattern: They were highly visible at one time because they were new, but as they become more commonplace, they become almost imperceptible. As Dennis Baron (1999, 2009) so aptly reminds us, at one time, pencil and paper was a new technology, but now it is invisible as a writing technology, allowing for certain kinds of composition to take place and not others. Pencil and paper is most often considered a nontechnology option for writing, even though it is as much a writing technology as a word processor.

The critical interest around directed self-placement (DSP) during the late 1990s and early 2000s serves as an example of a technology that receives less critical attention now that is no longer new and yet is still an important technology to consider and examine critically. When Royer and Gilles (1998) first introduced DSP in *College Composition and Communication*, it received a great deal of warranted, critical attention. In the years following its initial foray into composition studies, several articles (Bedore & Rossen-Knill, 2004; Blakesley, 2002; Lewiecki-Wilson, Sommers, & Tassoni, 2000; Schendel & O'Neill, 1999), an edited collection by Royer and Gilles (2003), and questions and responses via online forums debated its use and helped with implementation. Since that early onslaught of critical response, however, the initial buzz and scrutiny has evened out, and yet there is no reason to believe that DSP is not as significant and used as much if not more than it was 10 years ago. While institutions and programs are using and modifying it in a variety of ways and for different purposes, it has faded from the intense gaze that often accompanies new writing assessment technologies. This is a natural cycle that many technologies follow. As the technology becomes more common and adopted on a larger scale, it tends to garner less critical attention, fading into a type of sheltered invisibility. If we can see that cycle over a relatively short 10-year span, imagine how much more powerful that phenomenon might be for something like SAT tests, which have been around in one form or another since 1926. It is easy to envision why for so many stakeholders, especially those one step or more removed from daily educational practices, rarely stop and think twice about standardized tests or the high-stakes decisions educators make based on the results.

A second way that technologies become transparent is through institutional acceptance. Once organizations adopt a particular writing assessment technology, it is likely to become accepted rather rapidly and soon fade from the scope of critical analysis. This past year I administered a writing assessment for incoming students who had low scores on their SAT verbal and thus automatically were placed into a type of remedial or basic writing program offered through the writing center. The exam, which has been around for about 10 years, is a 90-minute timed writing exam delivered during freshman orientation that is holistically scored by writing center tutors. Without commenting on the merits or problems with that particular model of assessment, I'll simply note that it has become nearly transparent in that short time period. Few faculty know or care about it. Neither administrators nor students ask about how it is read or, more important, if it is accurate or appropriate to place students into or out of a class based on its results. I'd argue that it is better than the former model—using the SAT verbal scores only—but it has become so regularized than no one stops to think about it or how it could be improved . . . except me. However, I'm acutely aware of how the attention I might bring to the exam might backfire, resulting in a regression rather than an improvement. In light of the latest budget cuts and savvy marketing of the writing portion of the SAT, I fear that bringing a critical light to the exam might take away several of the features that I think are best: that we design the prompt, that the essays are read by people who teach our students and know our curriculum, and that we determine the criteria by which to evaluate the essays. It could be worse and might be if I am not careful in how much attention I give it.

Many other writing assessments function in similarly invisible ways, remaining relatively unchallenged over the years of their use. Another example is the current letter system of grading that is simply an assessment technology, but it escapes the critical gaze of most educators and students because our institutions have adopted and used that framework for years, requiring us to work within it with relatively few exceptions.

We may attempt to subvert it in interesting ways, but most of us in the end have to assign a grade on this scale, or at least something akin to it. Every so often when we see grading systems that differ from the standard, we might think briefly about the influence of it on the current educational climate, but even that is short-lived for most of us because of our institutional affiliations. While the issue of how or what to teach in writing classes may be highly contested, once an organization with institutional authority adopts a particular stance on the matter, the technology is well on its way to becoming mainstream within the particular community and closely followed by a level of relative invisibility that effectively shuts down the productive dialogue surrounding it. I am not arguing that individuals cannot illuminate technologies that have become invisible; in fact, that is exactly what I am arguing that educators should systematically do and what we need to do with digital writing assessments while they are still young in terms of institutional entrenchment.

A third way by which technology receives relatively little critical attention and thus becomes transparent is other pressing concerns within a particular context that distracts attention away from the technology. Christina Haas (1996) explains that "the images seen by looking *through* technology may be distorted without looking *at* the technology itself in a systematic way" (p. xi). By that standard, writing assessments are especially vulnerable to transparency in response to the enormous economic, logistical, political, or pedagogical demands that surround them that in turn diverts attention away from them as social technologies and the decisions being made based on the results of the assessments. Because of the institutional and cultural demands for assessing student writing, assessing teachers, and assessing programs and institutions, assessment technologies are developed to meet those needs in timely, cost-effective ways.

Educators work within strict accountability systems in accreditation that require providing evidence of student-learning outcomes and quality enhancement plans (QEPs) that, while well intended, often result in mistrust of educators and devaluating of teacher expertise. Huot and Williamson (1997) suggest a responsibility model as an alternative to strict accountability measures that are often implicit in larger-scale assessments. However, when the economic, political, educational, or social goals eclipse a critical consciousness of the technologies being used to meet those goals, they can become inconsequential in relationship to those external concerns. If the primary goal in using a particular placement mechanism over another is to curb the ever rising price tag of assessing student writing, the economic concerns during these times of rapidly depleting budgets might unduly outweigh a fair, critical analysis of the assessment. If a reductive rubric, for instance, is used primarily so that responding to and grading of student papers can be done more quickly to manage and justify ever increasing class sizes, these constraints distract from the appropriateness of responding to student writing with that particular method. That is not to say that pragmatic and material concerns about writing assessments are not part of the larger decision-making process—in fact, questions of cost, time, and efficiency are part of the sustainability of such assessments—but they should not be the primary criteria for selecting an assessment. In reality, these logistic concerns cover myriad dreadful assessments, some with little energy being spent on developing alternate methods, instruments, and uses.

Keeping a critical gaze fixed on assessment technologies takes vigilance and is an essential responsibility of educators in our use of them. Writing assessments serve vital functions in teaching writing to students, but they should not be left unexamined for even short periods of time lest we lose track of them and they fade into the institutional woodwork.

MOVING BEYOND INSTRUMENTALISM AND DETERMINISM

Two prevailing assumptions about technology shape our understanding of writing assessments: (1) an instrumentalism that results in an understanding of technologies as neutral tools, or (2) a determinism that results in the technology's fading from critical view. Both promote unhealthy attitudes toward writing assessments as technologies. As she suggests in the subtitle to her book *Technology and Literacy in the 21st Century: The Importance of Paying Attention*, Cynthia Selfe (1999) argues that a critical consciousness of any technology is important because it provides an awareness of how the technology has been shaped by and is shaping human activities and environments. Selfe concludes with this warning: "Technologies may be the most profound when they disappear. But when this happens, they also develop the most potential for being dangerous" (p. 160). There are consequences to not paying attention, as we all too often see in the realm of writing assessment. But it is often easier not to pay attention, especially to older and more established writing assessment technologies, unless we make a conscious effort to pay attention to them by turning a critical eye to what they are and how they function within educational contexts. In the next chapter we will look at several technological narratives that stem from the cultural assumptions outlined in this chapter and the educational undertow that favors a technological approach to writing assessments leading us away from the goals and outcomes we have developed as a discipline over the past half century. However, instead of taking a type of neo-Luddite antitechnology perspective—which is one way to address these concerns all too common in English departments—the rest of the book addresses ways in which we can adopt a technologically informed perspective on writing assessment that can lead us in a productive direction to achieve the outcomes we have defined instead of working against us, our goals, and even our students.

Cultural Narratives That Characterize Writing Assessments as Technologies

Yes, I love technology
But not as much as you, you see
But I still love technology
Always and forever.

—from *Napoleon Dynamite* (film)

M UCH AS CULTURAL ASSUMPTIONS of technologies have been ingrained in our collective cultural consciousness and thus defined many ways in which we understand writing assessments, we have developed cultural metanarratives or grand narratives (Lyotard, 1979) that manipulate how we read ourselves into stories of writing and its assessment. Like the cultural assumptions examined in the previous chapter, technological grand narratives tend to be polarizing, one-dimensional representations, creating a divide between those who have an optimistic vision of technocracy and those with a more pessimistic outlook.

> Visions of technology have a long history of such binary thinking. The visions of technologies as life-transforming, in both transcendent and threatening ways, have been reiterated and embraced again and again throughout history . . . with new technologies taking the place of more established ones in a seemingly endless cycle. (Sturken & Thomas, 2004, p. 2)

This cycle exists for writing assessment as well, with each new technological development ushering in promise for some and doom for others. Writing assessments as technologies often get defined by simplistic, polarized cultural narratives that do not account for the complexity of the authentic contexts in which writing assessments function. These grand narratives feed into the cultural assumptions that in turn sustain the narratives in a self-fulfilling cycle. The rhetoric that surrounds these educational narratives often shape our acceptance or resistance of certain writing assessments, since they function as technologies. Once we move beyond the dichotomous grand narratives, we are faced with the challenge—but also the opportunity—to rewrite our relationships with writing assessments and examine the accuracy and appropriateness of the decisions we make based on assessment technologies. First, though, we will want to understand narratives and their influence on our thinking about writing assessment.

TECHNOTOPIC NARRATIVES OF WRITING ASSESSMENTS AS TECHNOLOGIES

Especially within Western culture, technological advances have been inextricably related to the grand narrative of societal progress (Barton, 1994; Madaus, 1994; Winner, 1985). Since technologies are often understood as "advances" that convey such tangible benefits as simplifying, speeding up, amplifying, shrinking, and generally improving upon mundane human work and problems, new writing assessment developments often play into such values.

David Nye (2004) asserts that the utopian grand narrative of technology in the United States consists of three core beliefs: that technologies are a natural outgrowth of society, that they improve everyday life, and that they transform social reality (p. 171). Sometimes referred to as *technicism*— a term yet to be included in many dictionaries, but one I have encountered on several blogs and elsewhere on the Internet—this belief espouses a type of false hope or promise that technological innovations are propelling us in mostly constructive, mutually beneficial directions. Usually presented with a critical edge, *technicism* is often used similarly to Stanley Fish's "theory hope" (1987): something that promises much but doesn't live up to the expectation. Cultural displays of technicism can be seen in many examples, but few are as enjoyable as a *Saturday Night Live* sketch in which someone impersonating Steve Jobs introduces a series of new iPods, each getting smaller but with increased capabilities to hold music and other forms of media. The skit starts with Jobs introducing a new iPod he calls the "micro" that holds 50,000 songs on a device not much larger than a stick of gum. Immediately after introducing it, however, he throws it aside, proclaiming that the "micro" is now obsolete and proceeds to launch an even smaller iPod—the "pequeno"—that is even smaller and can hold a million songs. But alas the "pequeno," too, becomes obsolete only seconds after he introduces it, leading to the sketch's finale, an iPod so small it cannot be seen—appropriately named "invisa"—that holds 8 million songs and "every photo ever taken." The humor in the sketch is predicated on the audience's identifying with the cultural narrative that new, improved technologies are being introduced at an ever increasing rate but also the feeling that whatever technologies we purchase will be outdated almost as fast as we can open a new line of credit for a discount on our purchase. As we laugh we should also consider the absurd extremes in the promises of newer, better technologies being marketed to fulfill our insatiable appetite, which in turn feeds the technotopic grand narratives that are pervasive in our culture.

We certainly do not lack new technologies in writing assessment or their promises of reform and transformation of the work in which we engage. This can be seen not only in the marketing claims of assessment technologies from publishers and big testing companies but also in the scholarly reception of technologies even within the discipline. Natalie Syzmanksi (2010), in her presentation at the Conference on College Composition and Communication on the representation of technologies in the field through an empirical examination of the journals *Computers and Composition* and *College Composition and Communication*, reveals the tendency in our discipline to first introduce a technology with much fanfare, which is only then followed by research and critical theory, which provides a richer context for the initial optimistic narratives. Encouragingly, Syzmanksi's study shows a shift in recent years to representations of all three simultaneously when a new technology is covered by the major journals of our field. So while the technotopic narratives still exist, they may be more immediately tempered by critical research and theory.

The scholarship on writing assessment technologies often follows a similar pattern: claims that begin by extolling the benefits of a new technology followed by an acknowledgment of potential drawbacks or problems. Even this more critical view, though, can be disingenuous. Ellen Barton (1994) warns of this in what she calls the "antidominant view of technology" that is more critical on the surface level, but most often concludes that the benefits of a new technology outweigh the drawbacks, thus ultimately buying into the narrative of progress, even though it gestures toward a more critical stance. In writing assessments, portfolios demonstrate this pattern of reception. Early accounts of writing portfolios tended to wholeheartedly embrace the new assessment technology (Belanoff, 1994; Belanoff and Elbow, 1986; Murphy, 1997; Sommers, 1991). Initial claims included little serious critique or attention to potential drawbacks that might result from this type of assessment technology. Only after the widespread acclaim and acceptance of portfolios, the scholarship began to present more nuanced views and more cautious assertions. Once the assessment technology was forced onto students and teachers uncritically in ways unimagined by its early advocates, some of the same voices that were its proponents began to assert a more critical stance. Pat Belanoff (1994), for example, warns, "In truth, portfolios are not a cure-all; they are not going to magically make students better writers" (p. 20). Others, such as Murphy and Grant (1996), reflect on the rise of portfolio popularity in the 1980s and the pitfalls that often accompany such widespread acceptance of an assessment technology. Portfolio assessment scholarship then entered what Barton would label the "antidominant" phase of the technological narrative, which included a recommendation for adoption that remained the same, though they included critiques. Ultimately, though, portfolios remained accepted within teaching communities as beneficial if they were implemented and used correctly.

I point this out not to call into question the scholarship on portfolios or to suggest that they don't have important potential in writing instruction. I use portfolios in nearly all my classes and for my own scholarship as well. Rather, I wonder aloud to challenge us to consider what extent even we as writing experts are unduly influenced by the allure of technotopic grand narratives. They are particularly appealing to those of us who labor often with little external reward or encouragement, since they often affirm the effectiveness of our work to improve student writing.

The history of portfolio assessment speaks to the dangers of uncritical acceptance of a technology as being essentially beneficial to a community. While portfolio assessment can benefit students and our assessment of their writing, its widespread acceptance and application demonstrate the powerful technotopic forces that technologies tend to hold within educational settings. I don't believe that portfolios are an exception in this case. It seems that many, if not most, other writing assessment technologies (e.g., holistic scoring, timed writing tests, directed self-placement, grading rubrics, and now a second wave of portfolios with the ePortfolio) have followed a similar pattern: beginning with optimistic claims, followed by a more critical gaze, and resulting in the conclusion that the assessment is more beneficial than harmful for the community at large.

A core tenant within the technotopic narrative is that of efficiency. In a society that applauds overcommitment, busyness, and quick results, efficiency has emerged as one of technology's chief benefits. If a technology achieves efficiency, often regardless of the cost, it simply must represent progress, since the promise is that it will therefore allow people to fill their lives with something else, something more important or enjoyable than what the technology helps them accomplish. Be they kitchen appliances, direct-deposit checks, course management systems, handheld video games, or the latest digitized writing assessment, technologies are often marketed as a way to more quickly and efficiently complete mundane tasks in order to free up more time for more satisfying and important tasks. As one might expect, American educational systems, with their decreasing budgets and personnel, are especially vulnerable to such promises of efficiency (Williamson, 1994). Because educators are expected to produce statistically verifiable results with increasingly diminishing financial resources, efficiency has become the language of educational assessment.

As the number of students increased in American higher educational institutions, so did the need for efficient writing assessments to handle the diverse masses of students who populate higher education. As Stanley Aronowitz (2000) remarks, "In 1997, the proportion of college students to the adult population had risen to 13 percent, more than four times what it was in 1941. Of a work force of some 114 million, more than 15 million people of working age were enrolled in an institution of 'higher' learning" (p. 2). The latest economic downturn has no doubt increased the number of applications to higher education as well, and yet we are required to continually assess student writing regardless of how many students are in our classes or what their preparedness and goals for writing may be.

In much of the scholarship on new writing assessment technologies, authors commonly cite the time-consuming nature of large-scale and classroom writing assessment as rationale for adopting new technologies. That's the almost sinister beauty of the SAT verbal writing assessment. At a time when resources are scarcer than ever, an efficient writing assessment appears that shifts the financial burden away from institutions, though this burden is shifted to the shoulders of students. Even though Educational Testing Service (ETS) does not allow for independent verification of their systems, educators can't help but be drawn to it for its efficiency, despite deep misgivings. And those who know the most about writing assessment are often purposefully left out of the decision-making loop so that we don't unnecessarily complicate the technotopic narrative that those who control the purse strings so desperately want to believe.

Efficiency, though, is only a limited virtue in and of itself. Once efficiency is detached from related values such as objectivity and reliability, it has only temporal and economic consequences. If all else is equal, efficiency makes sense, but so often other, more important merits are ignored at the expense of efficiency. When the values synonymous with it are revealed to be deleterious to student learning, efficiency loses much of its educational appeal. On many fronts, educators continue to fight this battle, acknowledging the need for efficiency but advocating for other values that have a more significant effect on the quality of teaching and learning.

TECHNOPHOBIA: PESSIMISTIC NARRATIVES OF TECHNOLOGY

While many technological developments even in writing assessment are indeed remarkable, questions linger over such vexing issues as unintended consequences or side effects of new technologies; inequitable access and benefits of new technologies; and the idealistic promises of hope, happiness, and prosperity that often accompany new technologies. Once the early promises regarding the technology do not come to fruition or when the technology has been implemented for a long enough time that we become aware of some of its unintended social or educational consequences, we are still left with the work of teaching and assessing students who still struggle with their writing. This leaves us with a limited number of options.

The techno-enthusiast will probably move forward, nonplussed by the setback and ready to invest energy, time, and money in the next technology that seems most exciting and makes the boldest promises. Langdon Winner (2004) puts it this way: "Once the early returns have come in and the former seems tired and old-fashioned, the focus quickly shifts to other objects of fascination" (p. 37). Fortunately for the technophile, there are bound to be limitless new technologies toward which he or she may turn his or her attention, but the question of what happened to the former technology remains unanswered, as well as why we continue to believe a narrative that has so often been proved false. A more restrained approach may be to examine the situation to see where the technology fell short and was unable to deliver on its promises. Its potential is not lost, but it might take time to modify the instrument, technique, or process to see if there might be any appreciable improvements. While this moderate response may not be the subject of much critical attention, teachers do this regularly, probably more informally than formally, in something like the frame experiments George Hillocks (1995) discusses in *Teaching Writing as Reflective Practice*, where a teacher modifies an assignment or technique in an attempt to informally measure an appreciable change in the outcome (pp. 32–37). Another understandable response is to become skeptical toward technologies. Educators who have taught for a number of years and over that time bore witness to the unfulfilled assertions of new writing and assessment technologies to improve student writing or their teaching of writing may have the most reason to distrust the promises of yet more technological fixes.

Those who traditionally have been least served by educational institutions may be similarly disenfranchised by the grand claims of new educational technologies, especially those relating to writing assessment. Overwhelmingly, students of color, women, those from families with lower incomes, and those whose parents are least educated have the most right to be suspicious of claims associated with a new educational assessment. This in part results from new assessments being measured against the old ones in order to ensure their accuracy. For example, the

SAT writing exam claims that it produces results that are statistically consistent with its predecessor, the multiple-choice test (Kobrin, Patterson, Shaw, Mattern, & Barbuti, 2008). That's good news, of course, only if you believe that the old results were fair and unbiased in the first place. Students who have been disadvantaged by standardized tests for years find little encouragement in knowing that the new test will produce statistically similar results.

Since writing assessments typically reflect the biases of the culture in which they operate, they rarely if ever advantage minority populations. These biases can manifest themselves in a variety of ways within educational and assessment contexts. Jencks (1998) in "Racial Bias in Testing" classifies several types of test bias: label, content, methodological, and prediction.

Label bias is analogous to truth in labeling in the food industry or other consumer product businesses. While manufacturers of food and other products are obligated by law to clearly represent the contents of their products to consumers, test developers are not so obligated and as a result often seriously misrepresent their products. Content bias occurs when the questions or prompts favor a particular group over another. For example, if I am developing an essay prompt for placement of incoming students that centers around a local controversy or event, it will be biased toward students from the region where that issue received the most attention. Imagine writing prompts, for example, around subjects like racial profiling in Arizona, national trade policies with Cuba, or health care options for the poor. Each of these prompts might advantage some and disadvantage others based on how relevant that particular issue might be in the student's home community. Often in assessment situations students are not allowed to do outside research but must rely on prior knowledge to generate ideas for the test. Content bias is becoming more relevant as the debate over educational content continues to expand the scope of knowledge, information, and skills that are considered educationally appropriate. Methodological bias is when a test advantages one way of thinking or responding over others. The most obvious form in educational testing is the multiple-choice question. I know that in my experience I outperformed other students who may have known more than I did or studied harder simply because I knew the art of beating the multiple-choice test. American educational assessments have tended toward methodologies that value quick thinking, identifying the "best answer" among a list of possibilities, linear thinking, single correct responses, and factual recall. In fact, even though I consider myself weak in math and only average at logic, I consistently scored higher on computation than verbal on standardized examinations, since I could study and memorize formulas and patterns associated with those sections in ways that I could not do with the verbal section.

Finally, prediction bias occurs when a test is used to predict an individual's future performance, but that prediction disadvantages certain populations over others. While predictive validity is regularly dismissed by dominant voices in writing assessment (see any number of Ed White's posts on the Writing Program Administrator's Listserv over the past several years for examples), it is certainly reasonable to determine a test's ability to accurately predict future performance as part of a larger validity argument, especially when the results of that test are used to determine access to educational opportunities. While predictive capabilities alone are insufficient, as a part of a larger construction, they become a single but necessary component of validity. Because of the high-stakes decisions made based on it and the amount of research published on it, the SAT once again serves as a poster child for this issue, showing that the SAT is not an accurate predictor of college success for female, Hispanic, or African American students (Jencks, 1998; Garcia & Pearson, 1994; Shepard, 1993). A difficulty with the predictive nature of writing assessments is that the performance being measured on the test is often significantly different from those required to succeed in future performances. The skill and knowledge sets required to effectively write for 90 minutes by hand in an auditorium in the middle of summer orientation differs significantly from what students are required to do in a 1st-year composition class. Answering multiple-choice questions on the literature portion of an advanced placement (AP) test is even further removed from writing in 1st-year composition class. Yet both assessments often dictate the writing course that students might take or for which they might receive credit. The more closely the predictive assessment mirrors the targeted skills or knowledge base, the better the chance that the outcome will provide information that will allow assessors to accurately and appropriately predict future success, another reason that the SAT and similar assessments are a poor choice for making high-stakes educational decisions.

Test bias, however, is only one force behind the negative narratives of writing assessment. Another is that people have relinquished control and decision making to technologies (Turkle, 2004), a pattern that at least has some merit in the narratives of writing assessment. Luddites have become a symbol of active resistance and skepticism out of the assumption that technologies are working against human interests. While the original Luddites were a group of 19th-century English workers famous for their destruction of machines that threatened to replace them in the workplace, they "were themselves technologists—that is, they were skilled machinists and masters of certain specialized *technes* (including the use of huge, heavy hand shears, complicated looms, or large, table-sized cropping or weaving machines), by which they made their living" (Jones, S., 2006, pp. 3–9).

I would suggest that many of the neo-Luddites within our own discipline reflect a similar technological bias. Instead of being antitechnology, they are merely invested in older technologies in which they have developed expertise and that have afforded them accomplishments and gave them standing within the community. What may appear on the surface to be a staunchly antitechnological stance is simply a preference for older technologies. This is an important distinction here as well as in the second half of the book. Our options as educators are not between using technologies or not using them to assess student writing. Instead we choose between the types of assessment technologies we will use. A non-technological option does not exist. Writing assessments are bound to evolve, as does language, writing, and every other technology. That doesn't mean that we should be fatalist determinists and allow every new technology to define what we do and how we do it. Rather, as I will develop in the next chapter, we need to take an active role with the technologies, keeping up with the possibilities and shaping their development and implementation as much as it is in the best interests of our students to do so. When technophobic narratives abound, we lose focus of what might be done with assessment technologies that might help us achieve our goal in effectively providing feedback to students about their writing so they might have the best chance to learn and improve.

TOWARD A MORE BALANCED APPROACH TO TECHNOLOGY

Since educators regularly interact with technologies as a means to accomplish our teaching and administrative responsibilities, we are better informed about technologies when we choose to approach them outside the conditioned responses that these polarized narratives lead us. Educators rarely succeed when enticed by all the newest assessment or pedagogical technologies, uncritically accepting them as progress, or by looking through the technology at the goals we attempt to achieve with them. We are similarly ineffectual when we reject new technologies out of hand or choose to remain ignorant of new technologies that might push us beyond the skills and knowledges that have been foundational to our scholarship and teaching. Both methods lead to the same place—an uncritical and unaware stance toward technologies and their ideological ramifications. Writing assessments are specific types of technologies that are especially important to examine critically because they have such a profound influence on education.

CHAPTER 3

Decision Making and Development
of New Assessment Technologies

> Technology is dominated by two types of people: those who understand
> what they do not manage, and those who manage what they do not
> understand.
>
> —Archibald Putt

M ANY OF THE ASSUMPTIONS and narratives covered in the previous
chapters position teachers and students in passive roles. Because
educators have largely failed to anticipate and thus get out ahead of new
assessments and because we have largely abdicated the work of assessment developer/designer to technical experts rather than writing experts,
we are often left merely to react to—most often against—writing assessments that are foisted upon us. To be fair to us as teachers, though, most
educational environments have moved decisively to ensure that classroom
teachers do not have the authority to make important educational decisions
in relation to students and their writing. Statewide assessment systems at
the secondary level implemented in the No Child Left Behind era resulted
in heavy, top-down standardization of learning and accountability of teachers and schools. College writing, too, has suffered in recent years, with more
courses being taught by faculty, who often wield less authority to make
decisions and shape curriculum. Too often, teachers and schools—when
they have choices at all—face the difficult dilemma of either accepting or
resisting available assessment technologies over which they have had little
input in developing or choosing for their local site. That is not to say that
teachers have not done remarkable work within the limitations of existing
assessments or that a few of us have not been involved in the design, development, and implementation of some of these new technologies. However,
teachers rarely get the opportunity to assert a vision, shape the content, and
design writing assessments before they are made available.

At times we have relegated these formative and developmental roles
to technicians whose visions, limitations, and needs in turn trump the

values we might associate with the teaching of writing. At other times we have been purposefully and conspicuously left out of the process, even though we would like to participate. I recall an event hosted by a regional affiliate of the Writing Program Administrators in which a member of the College Board was invited to talk to us about the then new written portion of the SAT Verbal exam after it had been designed and was being launched. After presenting his sales pitch without any awareness of the increasing irritation of his audience, he opened the floor to discussion, feedback, and questions. Let's just say that he received quite a bit of each. Perhaps one of the best comments of the night came when a colleague pointed out that around the room sat a number of experts in writing, teaching, and assessment—many of whom were leaders in the field—and yet even though they claimed to include educators outside their organization, there were no systematic attempts to include, make common cause with, or solicit feedback from recognized experts and organizations of teachers.

The opportunity has been there, but no large-scale communication takes place until we are called upon to implement and use the assessments. In perhaps the most high-stakes writing assessment in the country, those of us with expertise in teaching students are not at the table until after the assessment technology has been released for our and our students' consumption. While we often make the best of challenging situations, we need to change our approach so we can be at the table earlier in the conversations and development of writing assessment technologies. By understanding the roles teachers can play, we can move toward more acceptable outcomes and consequences of writing assessments, instead of allowing the cultural assumptions and narratives explored in the previous chapters to exert unwarranted influence and control over assessment decisions.

In my first semester as a program administrator, I received a message informing me that our campus had recently adopted a popular course management system that had, among other features, an electronic portfolio platform that we should use in the writing program. Upon investigation of the system, it was instantly clear that it was of the reductive, drag-and-drop ilk designed for institutional data mining. Furthermore, I was informed that the institution also invested in the expensive and popular plagiarism-detection program I referred to in the previous chapter. One might have thought that as the director of 1st-year composition, I or my predecessor might have been part of the decision-making process for these adoptions. First-year writing had the most extensive electronic portfolio system in the university and our program produces far more student essays than any other in the university. However, the decision had already been made and the money spent long before. And, wouldn't

1st-year composition want to be the first to use the new electronic portfolio platform? It is supposedly so easy, and it centralizes control of content and design, which they assume is necessarily a helpful feature. It provides access to student data from which the college hoped to launch a university-wide general education assessment. Perhaps, they suggested, they could take a few hours during my often appropriated summer orientation to make sure all the writing teachers were "on board" with the new systems.

First, I made sure I was still breathing. My mind raced about how I would boldly resist, or at worst broker a compromise that would show a willingness to participate in university initiatives while keeping the integrity of our current ePortfolio system and yet shielding the writing teachers from hours of technological "retooling" that might be necessary for this adoption. Even though I eventually made peace with a kind of compromise that gave students an option of portfolio platforms to use, I wonder what alternative, and more effective, role I should have played in the process.

In this process, there are at least three stages during which those of us with writing expertise and teaching experience should exert influence for new assessment technologies: implementation, prediction, and design.

IMPLEMENTATION

For many of us, this sphere of influence is decidedly less expansive than for others. At least to some degree, though, we all exercise at least some agency in our classes, even if we gain some of this subversively. Although many teachers are held to strict measures of accountability—regularly submitting lesson plans with evidence of connections to state standards at the secondary level or standardized syllabi, textbooks, assignments, or rubrics at the postsecondary level—we still make choices daily in the classroom. We decide how to present ideas, what to emphasize, and what exceeds the required materials. Other teachers have much more agency to include content, delivery, goals, and assessments in the class. Still fewer of us have decision-making authority or influence over multiple classes in grade levels, programs, schools, departments, centers, and curricula. We all exercise some authority when we make decisions about which assessment technologies to use in order to make specific decisions about students, teachers, or programs.

In the classroom this plays out in any number of ways: in what technologies are necessary to complete the assignments, with which technologies (high or low tech) we choose to deliver course content, with what assessment mechanism we use to respond to and grade student writing.

For example I have a favorite assignment that I call the "monument/memorial re-design project," developed from a previous edition of Bedford/St. Martin's *Convergences* textbook. In this assignment students select a monument or memorial and do a number of smaller projects, leading up to a larger final construction piece. First, they need to take or collect pictures of the monument or memorial from multiple perspectives, which we connect to Burke's (1966) linguistic concept of terministic screens that reflect, select, and deflect realities (p. 46). Second, they analyze its rhetoric and reflect on how it communicates meaning to different audiences. Third, they critique its design. Then they make a model that represents a re-design of the monument or memorial. This final stage of the project is "open media," requiring students to select the medium to use for the re-design.

Some students construct it virtually within a range of digital software technologies to which they might have access and some level of proficiency. Some draw and/or color in the two-dimensional space of paper, while others construct three-dimensional models in anything from cardboard to clay to Legos. They select the medium, which in turn influences the range of possibilities I have for my response. While I might be able to write of the back of a paper drawing, I would need to find something different for the three-dimensional projects.

The same is true of the digital models, each of which presents certain opportunities while precluding others. I do not have to match my assessment medium to theirs—I could write paper responses or e-mail to them all regardless of media—but the point is that the choice of media and technology platforms in which we teach, compose, and respond are part of the meaningful, rhetorical decisions we and our students make regularly. While that has always been a possibility, I do not believe that has always been the norm. For many years school-based writing has largely been papers with written responses on them. New technologies are pushing up against those norms and making media visible in ways it may not have been for some time. While choices of media are not necessarily right while others are wrong, we will be compelled, I believe, to consider ways the medium allows for and disallows, emphasizes and deemphasizes certain communication in different rhetorical contexts.

Cynthia Selfe (1999) reminds us that choosing high or low tech options is not the real issue. Those who tend toward early adoption of technologies can be just as complicit in ignoring the ideology of technologies as those who chose to ignore them, and both lead to not paying critical attention to the technology (pp. 37–38). We may not always be happy with the choices we have at our disposal, but we need to determine which writing and assessment technologies will provide the best opportunities for teaching and learning in order to measure student performance and support them to improve their writing.

PREDICTION

Ultimately, we want to get out in front of new technological developments and exert some influence over them rather than merely making do with what is made available to us. Therefore, it is essential that we do a better job of predicting the trajectories of new assessment technologies. If we are accurate in our projections, we can be prepared to communicate our values as writing, teaching, and assessment experts more successfully. So often in writing, we are so busy with the day-to-day work of teaching, research, and service that we spend relatively little time thinking ahead to what writing assessment technologies might look like 5, 10, or 20 years out. We are relatively good at historicizing from where we have come (Hanson, 1993; Huot & Neal, 2006; Norbert, 2005; Yancey, 1999), and sometimes histories are positioned in the context of future projection. However, we have not done as well at learning from those histories to anticipate ways that writing assessment technologies will likely progress, thus reinforcing our position as reactive and a step behind. Ron Westrum (1991) asks four questions about technology more generally that might help us better predict potential writing assessment technologies as well:

1. How will the technology evolve?
2. What will the technology be used for?
3. Who will technology's users be? and
4. Who will decide how the technology will be used? (p. 335)

As we respond to these questions, we might begin to see where we can assert influence earlier in their developmental stages as well as become better at predicting places and contexts in which new writing assessment technologies might be foisted upon us. How the technology will evolve is the core question. Inasmuch as assessment technologies are built upon one another and are developed in response to perceived needs within communities, we can begin to forecast what to expect. One problem in predicting the evolution of writing assessment technologies is that we do not always account for educational changes: the students, the teachers, and the ratio between them; the changing purposes of secondary and higher education;

the changing political and economic landscapes; the changing organization, structure, and administration of our institutions; and other salient
factors. As Susan Oliver (1994) suggests, "Technology forecasters take a
rigid, simplistic view similar to the economic forecasters" (p. 47), and so
do we when it comes to assessment technologies. When we do look forward, we have so many factors to account for that it becomes increasingly
difficult to imagine what our classes, our students, or our work will look
like in 10 to 20 years. It is difficult to set goals and develop strategies for
the future when we are consumed by reacting to our current crises. As
underresourced and overworked as we are, it is hard to imagine freeing
up the time and energy to do anything but live in the present and do the
best we can for our students within the current situation.

Although we may derive only a little comfort in knowing that we are
not alone in our failure to accurately predict change, the magnitude of
missed projections is staggering in ways that are almost humorous:

> In 1913, the fledgling Mercedes Benz Company produced a forward projec-
> tion looking at motor car usage in 50 years time. They predicted that, glob-
> ally, there would be two million cars on the roads, based on the rationale that
> it would be too difficult to educate large numbers of people to drive. By 1950
> there were 50 million, and by 1989 555 million, vehicles worldwide. (Oliver,
> 1994, p. 50)

Despite the severity of its missed prediction, Mercedes Benz has done
rather well, but we cannot rely on similarly fortuitous mistakes to guide
our future. If we have a vision for providing higher education to increasingly diverse student populations, what should we expect of students,
teachers, content delivery, administrative structures, and writing and
assessment technologies?

Perhaps most important from the example above is determining what
our misguided rationale might be. What can't we imagine? Virtual schools
without physical buildings? Delivering course content in multiple languages? Writing and technological needs of future students? Machines scoring
student writing that will allow class sizes to grow astronomically? If we cannot imagine education changing in significant ways, we are most certainly
not able to anticipate what the teaching of writing will look like in years to
come. The only thing we can be relatively certain about is that it will change,
so what are we doing to prepare for that? While much of our time and energy
goes toward resisting change, it happens nonetheless and teachers are often
not the people with most influence over how or why it changes.

While teachers of English and college writing have made moves
toward shaping educational conditions and content in terms of position
statements on everything from "Student Rights to Their Own Language,"

published in 1974, to over 15 other position statements currently published on the National Council of Teachers of English/Conference on College Composition and Communication Web site (http://www.ncte.org/cccc/resources/positions), the statements tend to focus on current principles and practices rather than providing a vision for the future. Perhaps we need to charge an ad hoc committee to do just that: projecting and predicting the future needs of writing instruction at the secondary and postsecondary levels, to develop long-range goals, and to make recommendations—including those for assessment technologies—that would position us to meet them.

David E. Nye (2004) has several propositions that might guide a committee with such a charge:

1. *Prediction is difficult, even for experts.* Predictions can be difficult in part because market trends are complicated, and otherwise promising technologies can easily fail. Even with writing technologies, a product or method that appears to have enormous potential does not guarantee its success. Craig Stroupe (2000), for example, points out that many writing experts predicted hypertext to be the most significant force in digital writing, underestimating the value of hypermedia. Much of the early work in hypertext centered on linking texts and developing blocks of texts with multiple, nonlinear arrangements. It is this type of linked texts that I believe Jay David Bolter was referring to in his 2008 Computers and Writing keynote address when he said that "hypertext is dead." Few would have accurately predicted the relative viability of hypermedia and the relative stagnation of hypertext even a few years ago, except perhaps those who predict this kind of failure with all new technologies. A popular story on my wife's side of family is that her grandfather accurately predicted that they would be robbed when they were out of town on a particular vacation. The story concludes with the joke that he made the same prediction every time he went out of town. Those of us who routinely predict that each new technology will change the face of writing—for good or ill—are bound to be right part of the time. The trick is to figure out which is which and react accordingly.

   Adding to the increased difficulty in prediction for writing assessment technologies is the ever changing student populations, the (un)availability of technologies, the changing curricula, changing pedagogical practices, changing settings of teaching (e.g., distance education and hybrid classes), changing class sizes, and changing state standards and assessments. Even testing companies have begun to adjust to the digital age, having been reticent to make such concessions earlier. On the written component of the SAT Verbal, the following constraints are currently placed on students as they write: They are limited to 25 minutes to complete the entire essay; they are required to complete the essay in pencil ("Off topic essays, blank essays, and essays written in ink will receive a score of zero"); no students are allowed to compose on a computer; students have no access to research or resources during this assessment; and the writing samples are holistically scored by calibrated raters with no connection to the students, their goals, or their current educational contexts. This disproportionately influential writing test is the antithesis of nearly every current theory of composition and writing assessment and does not take into account the composing technologies students use in authentic environments. Yet it is inevitable that even the mighty Educational Testing Service (ETS) will have to acquiesce sooner than later and allow students to produce texts with at least word processing technologies. While that might be a small victory, I will posit my own prediction that is far less optimistic: Either while or shortly after they allow students to compose on computers, they will adopt machine scoring of student writing samples. They will make the "concession" not out of any desire to deliver authentic writing assessment but because it will be the most economically viable, and they can use the one as a smoke screen for the other.

2. *New technologies are market driven.* Markets have more to do with the development and implementation of technologies than most other factors, even though educators tend not to think in these terms. In other words, technologies will largely succeed or fail based on how they capture the imagination and needs of consumers. Nye (2004) illustrates this point with the forces that propelled the drug Viagra in the marketplace. Originally developed to treat a heart condition, called angina pectoris, in which the heart does not receive a sufficient blood supply during physical activity, Viagra initially did not include any reference to erectile dysfunction. Obviously, that is no longer the case, as consumers have driven the sales and alternate marketing and repurposing of the pill. The history of communication technologies is filled with similar accounts of consumer-driven markets that developed aside from their initial intent or expressed purpose: the telegraph, telephone, phonograph, and personal computer were all understood as curiosities with unclear commercial value, but consumer markets developed to drive their demand and production.

How might market demands evolve for writing assessment technologies if we were to make a concerted effort to support other assessments than those passed down to us by testing agencies? In part, this is what the state of California did when it exerted pressure by not using SAT scores for college admissions. If large groups of teachers and organizations made alternative assessment decisions in our own spheres of influence, we might see bigger markets for technologies other than the cookie-cutter electronic portfolio system, the plagiarism-detection software, or the books with writing exercises for students that we too often see. Conversely, the proliferation of reductive assessment technologies is based in part on consumer demand. Because of the decentralization of decision making and the ideology of academic freedom, we rarely think along the lines of collective efforts to develop markets for better technologies.

3. *Innovations proliferate rapidly.* Once a particular technology is available and a market develops for it, innovations and variations on that technology abound during a relatively small window of opportunity. During this time of proliferation, consumers can communicate their needs and desires to the technology developers and designers. Here it is important to have a plan and a vision for what we want the technologies to do for us instead of limiting our imaginations to what is or was available. Working outside existing paradigms might be more challenging initially, but the proliferation phase might produce market conditions that would persuade companies and technical support staff to meet needs that perhaps had not been available when the initial technology was being developed. Now, they are motivated to develop a market for the technology. Once an assessment technology, such as an ePortfolio platform, has reached the proliferation stage—which it seems to have achieved; nearly every publishing company seems to be marketing one—teachers and administrators have the unique opportunity to communicate how we need the ePortfolio to function so that we are not stuck with the uninspired drag-and-drop programs attached to our course-management systems.

   Mass-market companies are among the least likely to work with and for us, since their organization is predicated on volume rather than localized service. They grant themselves permission to do as little as possible to make adjustments because they do not see customization as in their best interest. Institutions often lock themselves into exorbitant, long-term contracts such as the way we have shelled out incredible amounts of money to photocopy companies for frustrating and error-prone machines. When market conditions change (e.g., when schools see the wisdom in fewer paper copies and more electronic documents), so does our ability to ask for innovations and modifications to meet our curricular, pedagogical, and assessment needs. If I need an ePortfolio platform to handle multiple drafts, reflective commentary, or peer feedback in a certain way, the current market should be ripe to make such demands at least for a limited time while there is a proliferation of options available. Once I make a commitment to a platform, I am less likely to get the company to make adjustments based on my program's or my students' needs.

4. *Best design does not always win.* While we might initially assume that the best designed technology will ultimately capture the market, mitigating factors are often pitted against it. Nye illustrates this point with the Betamax, which was a better technology than VHS, and the Macintosh's superiority over the PC to illustrate how superior technologies either have lost or have a smaller market share than they deserve based on quality alone. A similar battle is waging now between Blue Ray, which is trying to capture the digital movie market from DVD technologies, based on the argument of quality. Cost is often a primary competing factor when it comes to the success of a technology, but others such as marketing, consumer attitudes, product placement, and sometimes sheer luck factor into the equation.

The same could be said of writing assessments that are well designed do not always "win" in our schools. Many more thoughtful assessment technologies have been developed by teachers, writing programs, and institutions than have been implemented or have survived. Or the better-designed writing assessment is implemented for a short time until the realities of budget constraints, personnel support, and institutional politics take over and ultimately outlast us and our limited resources. Lest it seems I am being too harsh on ETS, the SAT Verbal exam, or other mass-marketed writing assessments, its presence has the potential to undercut and undermine local writing assessment efforts that have been developed at institutions all over the country, especially in times of budget reductions. One of the best writing assessment designs that I have had the pleasure of working with was a portfolio assessment that used high school, state-mandated portfolios to place students into college composition. In this assessment we collected data each year about student performance, student satisfaction, and teacher satisfaction in order to compare the portfolio system to those placed by standardized-test scores. What we found was encouraging, and the portfolio placement system initially prevented the program from having to adopt the COMPASS, as was the requirement for other institutions. Ultimately, though, after 8 years the portfolio placement assessment gave way to personnel and cost constraints. We swam against the undertow for a time before the prevailing forces drove the program back to cheaper methods because they were available and the institution did not value assessing students in better ways. One of the most frustrating aspects of mass-marketed assessment technologies is that even though they are often inferior in every way, mitigating circumstances—especially that of budget constraints—often dictate that they will prevail over far superior options.

5. *Uses of new projects are hard to foresee.* Since uses of technology are difficult to predict, we can assume that people will forever use technologies for unforeseeable purposes in unexpected ways. Edison invented the phonograph to aid in dictating business letters, not to play back music. The Internet was developed as a cold war defense mechanism. While that complicates the undertaking of prediction in writing assessment, it also provides exciting possibilities, since writing teachers have a history of subverting technologies (old and new) and using them in creative ways to accomplish a vast array of goals. I have known teachers who take the outdated materials they are required to use and find the most creative ways to teach students. I have known teachers who have used the most limiting state standards and developed compelling lesson plans despite them. I have known teachers who have taken the plagiarism software mentioned earlier and use it as a learning tool for students, having the students run an assignment through the program before the paper is due to see where problems might exist in their paraphrasing or citations and have the opportunity to make the appropriate adjustments before submitting their essays for evaluation. I have known writing teachers who have used outdated software and computers in the most creative ways, pushing their limits far beyond expectations. Part of our disciplinary identity revolves around our ability to work under whatever severe limitations are placed upon us and still teach writing in inspired and creative ways that engage and capture the imaginations of our students.

In writing assessment, using existing technologies for new purposes is possible as well, yet in doing so we need to proceed with caution. Assessments are not necessarily portable. An assessment might work in one situation for a particular decision, but cannot necessarily be transplanted someplace else or for another purpose without consideration of the validity of the new decision or context. Unfortunately, some scholars in writing assessment seem to have a one-size-fits-all mentality for assessment. Using existing assessment technologies for new purposes is possible and even wise if it can be done in such a way as to pay attention to its validity.

DESIGN

If prediction can help us anticipate technological developments, larger questions remain. How are assessment technologies developed and by whom? The answer for teachers tends to be, "I don't know who designs and develops the assessment, but it's not me." While there are English teachers and writing specialists who design writing assessment, this work more often than not goes to people other than educators or those trained in writing. They are trained instead in the technology of assessment. Educators may all use assessments and feel comfortable critiquing, applying, or modifying existing assessments, but most of us do not see ourselves as active developers or designers of assessment technologies. Most assessment gurus are not necessarily the people who actually design and develop the new technologies. More likely they introduce us to or advocate for a method, or they might help us see how to frame information we collect in an assessment for different stakeholders. When it comes to digital writing assessments, the gulf seems even greater, since so few of us have expertise in coding or in programming languages that are often necessary to develop something like a new electronic portfolio platform. Yet the development and design of new writing assessment technologies does not have to be an individual effort. If they are considered more of a collaborative effort, we as writing experts have much to contribute in the process if we can determine when, where, and how to assert our visions for writing assessment.

It is important not to conflate the roles of designer and developer when dealing with new technologies. Those who initially create and develop technologies rarely have the last say over their final form. While writing faculty might not always have access to technology developers, opportunities exist for increasing interaction between designers and users if faculty are ready to speak to our values and needs. While in some cases the technologies are fairly far along in the developmental process, we still might be able to exert some influence over them prior to the technology being released, or in other cases, we may be able to get the technologies modified to meet local needs.

Writing experts are not always separate from the people who develop and design assessment technologies. In addition to writing textbooks, some of us work on software, Web applications, and management systems. Especially since digital technology development is not synonymous with writing code (though there are some of us who do that as well), we have more opportunities to work with programs that are more accessible to nontechnology experts (Hartley, Schendel, & Neal, 1999). It is not surprising that some of the very best technologies in the field have been developed by writing experts. Assessment designers and developers in the field will tend to frame questions and problems differently from those who are not (Huot & Neal, 2006). Those outside the field tend to approach writing assessments in response to cultural assumptions and grand narratives rather than through issues and motivations central to the teaching of writing. Notice some differences between the ways in which assessment problems can be framed, as shown in Table 3.1. These are only simplistic examples, but they represent values and assumptions by which different stakeholders approach problems and questions of assessment.

Because writing experts have a wide range of interests and our research, teaching, and service loads are not significantly decreasing, it is unrealistic to think that we can all develop expertise in writing assessment technologies, which is why sponsorship is so important in the development of effective writing assessment technologies. As Deborah Brandt

Table 3.1. Framing the assessment problem.

Frame	Core Questions	Student-Specific Question
Grades/ Scores	What formula or algorithm can we create that will assign a grade or score to a piece of student writing that is as accurate and reliable as a human reader?	What grade or score should I assign this piece of writing that will accurately communicate my assessment of this student's writing based on the criteria provided for successful writing?
Response	What technology can we develop that will minimize the time and energy it takes to respond to student writing?	What responses can I provide that will help this student understand the performance on this paper and help her learn about writing in order to apply it either in a revision to this piece of writing or in future writing situations?
Placement	What's the most efficient (time and money) way to get students into the appropriate first year composition class?	What information is available that will help me or this student select the writing class that will best fit her needs and maximize her ability to achieve the outcomes for the program?
ePortfolios	What system can we develop or adopt that will be easy for students to learn and from which it will be easy to collect assessment data for accreditation or other large-scale assessments?	What system can we develop or adopt that will encourage this student to engage in a full writing process, see connections between and among his or her writing samples, and provide flexibility in engaging in reflection that might appear in a number of different genres?

(2001) has defined them, in terms of literacy, sponsors are "any agents, local or distant, concrete or abstract, who enable, support, teach, and model, as well as recruit, regulate, suppress, or withhold, literacy—and gain advantage by it in some way" (p. 19). Sponsorship of technologies in general, and writing assessment technologies more specifically, become a critical component of their development.

So who are the groups or organizations that sponsor assessment technologies? As Brandt recognizes, literacy sponsors have agendas that they promote and by which they gain some advantage. So too do writing assessment sponsors, who at present tend to be administrators, corporations, testing agencies, and government entities. Not all writing assessments that are developed in response to these sponsors are necessarily bad, but we must acknowledge the agenda they bring to the table. These tend toward values that are in their own interests and not those of students and teachers: accountability, efficiency, ease, consistency, cost effectiveness, comparisons, data mining, and so on. These values stand in stark contrast to what students and writing teachers often want, namely, formative and summative feedback and evaluation of writing that will help students and programs improve. If we as writing experts don't have reasonable, sustainable sponsors of writing assessment technologies, it is unlikely that we will be able to sustain the momentum to make any significant, lasting change. The undertow will be too much for us. When we develop or find a great ePortfolio system, placement method, or response system, we need sponsors that are available, for example, educational organizations, publishing companies, writing programs, and institutions, and committed to supporting them so they have the best chance to survive. Also, when we have no sponsorship, we do not see the kinds of writing assessments that are consistent with our best understanding of language learning and writing pedagogy. That is largely the story of large-scale writing assessments today and one that needs to change as we move forward into a time of reform, when we reestablish writing assessment technologies for teaching and learning.

FINDING A PLACE AT THE TABLE

If technologies are merely tools, it hardly matters if we choose to forge ahead with some and resist others because we assume that once they are developed and distributed, we can control how they are used and implemented in the curriculum. It positions people as the primary agents of change through adoption or implementation of new technologies that are developed by testing of technology experts rather than by those with a disciplinary investment in the teaching of writing. If this is our vantage point, it is often difficult to determine the many unintended side effects of the assessment technologies, and even if we are aware of their potential harm, we may rationalize that no method is perfect and that inequities and (dis)advantages will ultimately work themselves out as the technologies become more accessible to all. In this model, people are assumed to be the primary agents with the power to determine and ultimately control the outcomes of using certain technologies for writing assessment.

In contrast, a deterministic model asserts that we can do little more than respond and react to new technologies that are foisted upon us with little if any control in their development and use. This seems too often to be the case with writing teachers, who tend to respond after the fact to many of the technologies that are available to us. In one camp the early adopters tend to be ready to be among the first to integrate new writing or assessment technologies into their courses. The other camp tends to abhor technologies, forgetting that the overhead, chalkboard, and book are as much technologies as SMART Boards, wikis, and text messages. For them, any online source is suspect, so it becomes easier to forbid online research rather than teach students to evaluate the merits of different types of sources. Those who position themselves against technologies often point out errors in digitally produced texts as proof that they are undermining writing, as if print texts from the same authors would be error free. Educators resist and often ignore new technologies as if their denunciation would undermine the technological movement. However, they have no more control over emerging technologies than the Luddites had over the machines that were replacing them in the textile factories.

Both these positions lead to the type of uncritical acceptance or rejection of technology about which Cynthia Selfe (1999) warns. The danger here is to become invested in one of the assumptions or narratives to the extent that we miss the opportunity to critically examine the technology. However, a commitment to these positions or narratives shouldn't shape our responses to new or old writing assessment technologies. We can and do exert a limited amount of control and agency in the development and use of technologies for writing or writing assessments. While we may not exclusively control the vast range of social, political, and educational contexts in which they function, we need not be defeatist in our attitudes toward technological developments that play out in the arena of writing assessments as well as any other sphere.

Writing Assessments with Technologies

The Mechanization of Writing Assessments with Technologies

Mechanization best serves mediocrity.

—Frank Lloyd Wright

THE FOCUS for the second half of this book shifts away from writing assessments *as* technologies to writing assessments *with* technology. In other words, while all writing assessments are technologies and thus function as such, writing assessments are also increasingly becoming, including, and using digital technologies. That writing assessments are increasingly adopting newer, higher-tech options is descriptive rather than evaluative. Digitalized writing assessments are not necessarily better than their lower-tech predecessors, nor should we fall into the trap of false nostalgia that assumes older ways of assessing writing are somehow purer and thus superior to newer methods. Each high- and low-tech writing assessment deserves its own consideration in light of the local context and what decision needs to be made based on its results. Some digital forms of writing assessment are more compelling than others, but that does not imply a sweeping generalization about the relationship between writing assessments and technologies.

Writing assessments *with* technology, regardless of the specific context and application, is worth deeper examination for at least three reasons:

1. Because digital developments in writing assessment are often promoted as part of a narrative of progress, educators need to develop a critical eye toward technical solutions to educational issues.
2. Because writing outside the classroom is increasingly digitalized and multimodal, teachers need to be knowledgeable of 21st-century literacies in order to determine what to include in their assignments, classes, and programs.
3. Because many students are now producing high-tech texts (Web pages, blogs, wikis, podcasts, digital videos, etc.) that invite

multimodality, if not in some cases necessitate digital technologies, teachers need to explore new ways of assessing writing.

As educators it is our responsibility to sort through the cultural assumptions and narratives about digital technologies to determine what the writing assessments with technology are actually measuring and promoting, to understand how high-tech assessment applications function, and to find ways to respond to the increasing body of student-produced digital texts.

Assumptions that newer digital technologies represent educational progress drive much of the marketing and technohype that surrounds "advances" in writing assessment. There seems to be an increasing buzz around such technologies as electronic portfolios, machine-scored student writing, and plagiarism-detection programs, albeit from different sources and for different reasons. They signal a type of promise that new technologies are apt to make: that they address a problem and can be used to make decisions quicker, more efficiently, and without the weakness of human subjectivity. Most important, they promise to make the educator's job easier by reducing the busywork that occupies time that could better be spent in more productive ways. While these claims appeal to various stakeholders, many high-tech assessments work directly counter to values of good writing, including an emphasis on rhetorical issues such as audience, purpose, genre, delivery, and arrangement. Additionally, newer, digital technologies can work against the core values that writing assessment experts within the field have identified. Brian Huot (1996b) summarizes these principles best when he identifies the following characteristics of effective writing assessments: site based, locally controlled, context-sensitive, rhetorically based, and accessible. One aspect of high-tech options is the mechanization of digital writing assessments. If this trend continues unchallenged, writing assessment and writing teachers will increasingly be at odds, which will not help students achieve the 21st-century literacies they need. As long as the digital assessment technologies are relatively new, we have a unique window of opportunity to revolutionize the way we see, implement, and use them to make important educational decisions more consistent with teaching and learning as we have come to understand them.

THE PROPENSITY OF WRITING ASSESSMENT
TO MOVE TOWARD MECHANIZATION

At the heart of much of the new work in writing assessment technologies is the propensity to move toward mechanization as a guiding principle. It is one of the most powerful forces in the undertow of educational and writing assessment culture and practice. Even before the digital revolution of which we are currently a part, mechanization in writing assessment was touted as a way to ensure consistency (i.e., reliability), objectivity, preciseness, and speed, long the hallmarks of "technological progress" in writing assessments. Central to this mindset are the mistrust of human decision making and the fetishization of objectivity and scientism that are common features of the psychometric assessment (Broad, 2003; Huot, 2002; Moss, 1994) and remain key components in many current models, which makes them particularly difficult to challenge and dislodge from their place of privilege. It is particularly difficult in our current climate to make arguments for writing assessments that may be better but may also be more expensive or time consuming. Those of us who care about the work being accomplished via writing assessments, however, think that the investment is worthwhile. When difficult decisions have to be made regarding budgets and personnel, human-based assessments are often seen as a place to cut, especially when mechanized options are available that have been deemed acceptable because of their high level of reliability.

Of the efforts to mechanize writing assessment before digitalization, none was more influential than the argument testing companies constructed for indirect over direct measures of writing. Since genuine student writing was not practical to collect and assess, multiple-choice tests on "related concepts" such as vocabulary, grammar and usage, and reading comprehension became a proxy, as they supposedly correlated with student writing. Indirect measures of writing, which produce such objective and reliable results, were and continue to be staunchly defended by testing companies. Even though they cannot be adequately defended to those of us who study and teach writing, they are used because they produce quantifiable results that are relatively inexpensive, consistent, and objective. Thus indirect measures have enormous ethos with the public and with many in educational circles. Even the SAT Verbal, with its nod toward direct assessment in recent years, is still two thirds indirect. The Educational Testing Service continues to cling to mechanized, indirect measures because they are needed to claim objectivity and reliability.

Despite the enormous power undergirding its structure, indirect measures have been seriously challenged in the past 2 decades (Camp, 1993; Moss, 1994; Smith, 1993; Wiggins, 1992; Williamson, 1994) since writing abilities cannot be adequately represented by isolated skills. In addition, indirect writing assessments undermine the complexity of literacy for both readers and writers, something that becomes of utmost value when we shift our attention toward digital writing:

> [Indirect measures,] despite their purported economy, efficiency, and objectivity, are seen as extracting a high price in terms of such effects on teaching and learning as the emphasis on isolated, low-level skills and the displacement of skills and strategies necessary to higher-order thinking, problem solving, and metacognitive awareness. (Camp, 1993, p. 62)

When it comes to making decisions about students' writing, educators want to see . . . student writing. It does not seem like an unreasonable request, but it has taken decades and enormous pressure to procure such results.

Directly assessing student writing, especially in large-scale contexts, presents the following obvious challenges:

- *Labor.* Who will assess the writing? How much time will it take?
- *Criteria.* Upon what will the evaluation be based?
- *Fairness.* How can we ensure that students will get a consistent reading and score as compared with other students?
- *Cost effectiveness.* How much will it cost in reoccurring dollars? Who is going to pay for it?

The answers to these questions, namely, of cost, will tell someone more about how writing—its teaching and assessment—is understood and valued by an institution. If the costs and personnel commitments are not shared across disciplinary, departmental, and college lines, eventually even those who most value the work done through the assessment may grow to resent it, since it is not valued enough by others to share the burden. Not coincidentally, the questions above mirror the marketing of highly mechanized writing assessments.

Even though a move in writing assessment was made to direct measurement, it immediately spawned mechanistic processes and procedures to protect itself from charges of subjectivity. Because of the need to circumvent accusations that an assessment decision is biased, mechanical objects and processes have served to provide a claim of impartiality. Writing assessment mechanisms such as rubrics and holistic scoring methods arise from dual concerns for direct and objective measures. In one of the best books that challenges the misnomer that large-scale writing assessments cannot cultivate complex, nuanced, and contextual evaluation of student writing, Bob Broad in *What We Really Value: Beyond Rubrics for the Writing Class* (2003) recounts the introduction of rubrics to large-scale writing assessment in 1961, a time he sees as the birth of modern writing assessment: "Rather than seek to understand and carefully map out the swampy, rocky, densely forested terrain of writing assessment found lying before them, they [Educational Testing Service and other commercial testing corporations] quickly moved to simplify and standardize it" (p. 5), which they did by defining seven characteristics of writing that could be isolated and measured.

In a system he calls *dynamic criteria mapping* (DCM), Broad challenges the simplification and reduction of writing that embraces the complex and fluid nature of writing and its evaluation. DCM's strengths are exactly what mechanization is not: human based, time consuming, labor intensive, rewarding, knowledge generating, tolerant of multiple ways to demonstrate competencies, and faculty development–oriented. As William Condon (2006) points out, faculty development occurs when faculty come together to collectively assess student writing (p. 215). The more diverse and cross disciplinary the faculty, the more benefit the writing assessment will have on faculty development. These conversations and the resulting internalization of criteria about effective or ineffective writing are perhaps the most rewarding aspects of working with writing assessments not present in mechanized scoring methods. Testing companies have no motivation to promote faculty development at our institutions, nor are they invested in conversations about the evolution of criteria and how that might affect our curricula. While they tout their mechanized assessments as freeing teachers from the mundane work of writing assessment, they do not acknowledge that in turn they are liberating faculty from valuable development opportunities, chances to learn about students, their writing, and writing programs at the institutions.

Among the most significant writing assessment technologies that allow for direct writing assessment is holistic scoring. While the details of individual models of holistic scoring vary across contexts, Ed White (1985) defines six elements of holistic scoring that, if observed, will result in high levels of reliability while still being cost effective:

1. Controlled essay reading: read at same time and place
2. Scoring criteria guide (called a *rubric*, otherwise known as *traits*)
3. Sample papers (sometimes called *anchor papers*)
4. Checks on the reading in progress
5. Multiple independent scoring
6. Evaluation and record keeping

While holistic scoring does not have to be highly mechanized, commonly its procedures are.

A notable except to this rule is Bill Smith's model of holistic scoring, which he modified at the University of Pittsburgh. This model differs from traditional holistic scoring in several significant ways.

First, instead of using a numbered scale with anchor texts and calibration, Smith developed a scale based on the courses and curricula in the writing program. Second, instead of the final decision being made based on a numerical average and disagreement between raters understood as error, his system allowed readers to reach different conclusions about the appropriate course by discussing and reaching resolution together. Third, instead of scorers being focused primarily on placing the text accurately on the scale (which becomes the most critical component of the assessment), his system acknowledged students as the central focus and acknowledged that their decisions about the students would have a direct impact on whether or not the students' needs were being served (Smith, 1993, pp. 142–205).

Most holistic scoring over the past several decades has not resulted in such carefully enacted procedures. Rather, much of the assessment methodology, which is as much a part of the technology as the instrument itself, promotes or is dependent on highly mechanized procedures, including calibration of scorers; disconnection between scorer and writer; interrater reliability as the guiding measurement of successful scoring (assuming that if two scorers agree, it must be the correct score); and the centralization of power and authority through selection of anchor texts, strict monitoring, and selection of criteria.

Looking at one of these procedures, the calibration of scorers, demonstrates how mechanistic processes and procedures dominate human reading and response. Anyone who has participated in highly mechanized holistic scoring sessions—and they can be found in contexts such as AP exam–scoring sessions, placement exams, and ePortfolio-scoring sessions—will recognize the process of learning to score rather than read a text. While some holistic readings can promote local, human, contextual decision making, most are functionally mechanistic. The difference comes in the way people are asked to read or score. Most holistic assessment includes calibration, in which, as the name suggests, assessors are trained to suppress their human reading and response habits in order to gauge their score consistently with predetermined and highly regulated criteria.

Having a rhetorical understanding of how writing functions in different contexts for different audiences and purposes does not help a person become an effective cog in the machinery of a highly mechanized holistic scoring session. I am skeptical of any writing assessment system that attempts to devalue the human response, expertise, experience, and agency of the reader in an attempt to standardize the procedure for the sake of consistency. Broad (2006) inventories significant capabilities of human readers that should not be overlooked in the assessment of writing or somehow squelched by the mechanical processes of scoring student writing:

- Rhetoric (performance and analysis)
- Feelings (curiosity, humor, irony, pleasure, desire)
- Human relationships in the learning and teaching of writing
- Diverse kinds of reading (poetic, perfunctory, generous, mean-spirited, imaginative, critical)
- Validity and educativeness

His response, though it is targeted at computer-scored student writing rather than holistic scoring, is nonetheless applicable to any highly mechanized writing assessment that at its core attempts to separate the humanity from reading, responding to, and evaluating writing.

THE PATH TO MACHINE-SCORED STUDENT WRITING

Although indirect measures and holistic scoring function as nondigital examples of the propensity within writing assessment toward mechanization, arguably the emergence of machine-scored student writing has become the most disturbing expression of that tendency. Note Carl Whithaus's (2006) warning against the wholesale rejection of mechanized writing assessments:

> I would respectfully want to argue that the Conference of College Composition and Communication's committee of Teaching, Learning, and Assessing Writing in Digital Environments has made a mistake by continuing composition studies' tradition of rejecting software as a reader, responder, and assessor of student writing. . . . What composition studies needs is not a blanket rejection of these systems but rather data-driven studies of how these different software agents are already being used in postsecondary writing courses. (pp. 175–176)

His warning, however, seems more targeted at understanding the range of digital assessment technologies, such as his example of how teachers use Microsoft Word's features to encourage sentence- and paragraph-level revision, rather than a defense of student writing being scored by a machine, which is the more common way of understanding machine-scored writing. Also, he does not acknowledge what is being communicated by promoting mechanized assessments, even on a smaller scale. Put simply, those of us who are well versed in grammar and correctness can use Word's spell and grammar checkers more effectively than those without that foundation. Some students can become even more confused by using the technology, since they do not have the critical capacity to distinguish false positives (things marked incorrect by the machine that are fine, such as sentences that are deemed by the machine as "too long," rhetorical uses of passive voice, or correct words that do not appear in the dictionary feature) and unmarked negatives (things that are marked correct that are not, such as homonyms, ambiguous statements, and incorrectly cited paraphrases). While we can use the technology as a teachable moment, it subtly communicates features of effective writing that are not in context and are often at odds with what we are teaching. It takes a knowledgeable and mature student to use the technology without at least in part buying into its assumptions.

The same is true of plagiarism-detection software. Beyond the often unacknowledged ownership issues and panoptic surveillance mentality, it takes a fairly disciplined and experienced teacher of writing not to use the technology in ways that reduce our best understanding of citation and documentation. Otherwise savvy teachers can be lured into a false sense of confidence or into a mode of complacency based on assumptions of the technology.

Based on a series of increasingly complex mathematical algorithms, computers are counting in more complex ways than ever before, which has resulted in the claim that machines can now "read" and score student writing as reliably as their human counterparts (the claim is often at 97%–99% consistency with human readers) but without all the baggage that human readers bring with them. The perceived benefits of machine-scored writing are clear and central to the mission of mechanization: "The scoring machines promise three things for your money, all explicit in the home pages and the glossy brochures of industry automated-scoring packages: efficiency, objectivity, and freedom from drudgery" (Haswell, 2006, p. 64). Despite the technological optimism of advocates—who are not surprisingly the same people and groups that have the most financially to gain from this technology—the response from writing teachers to computerized scoring reveals an impassioned rebuttal as seen in this often-cited passage from Anne Herrington and Charles Moran (2001):

> From our perspective, the replacement of the teacher as reader threatens not just our jobs—a real consideration—but seems likely to change our students' sense of what it means to write in school and college. More fundamentally, it defines writing as an act of formal display, not a rhetorical interaction between a writer and readers. (p. 481)

Their first concern, which I don't find compelling as a rationale, is that of job security. If teachers have no more justification for human assessment of student writing than the protection of our jobs, then perhaps we should turn in our red pens and concede our work to computer technologies. As developed in previous chapters, we certainly do not want to be the neo-Luddites of the 21st-century university workforce, fearful and in denial of the changing relationship between technologies and the work we do. However, there are other reasons to resist such a concession, as Herrington and Moran note in their second claim: that computerized evaluation changes the rhetorical nature of writing as an act of communication. The rhetorical nature of reading and writing is the hill on which teachers of writing should make our stand against the pervasive notion that machines can do the work of assessing student writing and that they can do it better since they are objective and reliable.

A fundamental question within this larger debate is what computers actually do with student texts as they score them. Can machines read student writing? In what sense? If computers read by counting, what exactly are they counting and how does that relate to human reading? How are they determining which score or response is most accurate or appropriate? Can machines be programmed to consider the larger decision that will be made based on the results? These and other questions are being pursued by writing experts to balance some of the claims currently provided by the organizations that develop them. Without seriously distorting the ways in which those within the discipline understand reading, computers can be said to count and calculate more than they can be said to read in a semantic sense (Hayles, 2002). Condon (2006) goes even further in clarifying what computers do when "reading," weighing it against a rhetorically meaningful act of textual engagement: "What we want to notice here is that the machine does not in any sense *read* a text. It simply searches for a feature (periodic sentences, conjunctive adverbs, topic-specific vocabulary, vocabulary or concept mapping, etc.) and assigns a score based on how many of those features it finds and how frequently it finds them" (p. 211). Only a few times in my life (and only as a researcher) have I ever processed a text in the way Condon describes of machines above; however, even in that context, I was coding a text within the framework of a discourse/text analysis methodology for a research project. For example, I have participated in a project in which I looked at student texts, counting the number and types of revisions students made based on feedback they received during peer evaluation sessions. Even in this situation, I do not believe a computer could have assigned the "type" of revision without having to reduce the concept to something quantifiable such as the number of characters that were changed or whether something was added to or subtracted from the text. My coding scheme was more complex and would have required human reading and interpretation. Still, I would be hard pressed to call my coding of a text a "reading" that in any way resembles what I do when making meaning through reading texts, as

Condon aptly notes. While the ways and the complexity of counting that computers can do with student texts may be impressive, I approach with skepticism any claim of "machine reading"—a term I purposely avoid in this book in response to the way I defined *reading* earlier—as should others who are considering any form of digitalized writing assessment. When companies bolster their use of machine scoring with claims of high levels of correlation with human readers, we should immediately see warning flags and remember the similar way they continue to promote indirect measures of writing in the face of all the arguments to contrary. The same logic and the necessity to promote their products are at work here.

Although the current manifestation of computerized scoring is relatively new and its increasing popularity is alarming, the argument for or against computer grading technologies is not new to writing assessment. Brian Huot (1996a) provides a brief history of the debate, starting in the mid-1960s when Ellis Page and Dieter Paulus promoted the use of computerized grading by arguing that writing could be broken down into small, quantifiable measures, such as punctuation, that computers could locate and evaluate (p. 232). As computer technologies became more advanced, the algorithms used to quantify writing could become more complex, increasing the list of initial target features for evaluating student writing (pp. 232–235). Assessors have been working with technicians to identify quantifiable elements of writing that could be processed, analyzed, and ultimately evaluated by computers that would correlate at high enough levels with human readers to ultimately become a substitute for them. As computer technologies become more capable of processing mass amounts of information quickly, claims about the superiority of machine-scored student writing grew stronger and attracted more attention, because of a number of features, not the least of which is the rising cost of education and the increasing number of students to assess.

Herrington and Moran (2001) name just a few of the most marketed computer grading programs, noting that many are currently being used in large-scale and classroom writing assessments. Knowing the products and their connections to organizations or institutions is important in the analysis of how they function and how they are promoted and adopted. They provide this useful, though partial, list of several of the most popular computer scoring technologies:

> E-rater, developed by Educational Testing Service (ETS), is today used as one reader for evaluating the essay portion of the Graduate Management Admissions Test—a human still the other reader. Intellimetric, developed by Vantage Technologies, is used for evaluating writing in a range of applications, K through college. WritePlacer Plus, developed by Vantage for the College

Board, is being marketed as a cheap and reliable placement instrument. The Intelligent Essay Assessor, developed by Landauer, Laham, and Poltz and the University of Colorado, is now being marketed through their company, Knowledge Analysis Technologies, to evaluate essay exams for college courses across disciplines. (p. 480)

Not surprisingly, the company's marketing plans spin the technologies in the most positive light, insisting that the technologies are designed to relieve teachers of the burden of student grading and evaluating. This logic perpetuates the assumption that teaching composition and reading, responding to, and evaluating student writing is drudgery, something to be avoided (or outsourced, as a colleague of mine once commented, regarding the composition program) rather than to be embraced as an essential and engaging feature of the discipline and the work we do as teachers of writing. In addition, it reduces the role of composition teachers and others who respond to student writing to a mechanized, menial task to be relegated to computer technologies, freeing educators to do the "real work" of the academy, which apparently is not done through writing assessment. Much as mechanized writing assessments steal development opportunities from faculty in large-scale writing assessments at institutions, they also threaten opportunities at the classroom level to use writing assessment as a place for dialogue and teaching (Huot, 2002, p. 133), which is fundamental to the way many teachers understand and value the teaching of writing.

Here is the crux of the issue: Assessment at its best is a rhetorical act regardless of the scale. A machine can emulate reading, response, and evaluation, but it is limited to discrete, quantifiable characteristics of counting features in texts, which reduces literacy to isolated skill sets. Regardless of their speed and reliability, machines cannot read in the same sense as a human reader. The battle between human- and machine-evaluated writing is a value judgment—that of subjective reading for meaning and content or objective counting of quantifiable elements.

Knowing that for educators meaning-making and reading for content will ultimately trump quantifiable issues such as spelling, word count, length of sentences, and correct grammar and punctuation, marketing for machine-scored writing assessments promote their ability to read and make meaning in texts, which should tell us something about the ethics of such marketing plans. Their advertising proves that the companies know what they need to measure even if they do not live up to the assertions they make. Patricia Freitag Ericsson (2006) shows the extent to which companies will go to manipulate language in order to make claims that their programs "almost read" as in the examples of Intelligent Essay Assessor, which cites the ability of their algorithm (note: a mathematical formula) to "accurately mimic human understanding of language," or IntelliMetric's claim that it is an "intelligent scoring system that relies on artificial intelligence to emulate the process carried out by expert human scorers" (Ericsson, 2006, p. 28). Emulation and mimicry of reading and understanding student writing are a far cry from a human reading.

Ericsson rightly notes that claims such as these are deceptive at best and purposefully misrepresent what they do in order to persuade the educators that the software can read, understand, and assess student texts in ways that are consistent with expert human readers. She provides below one of the best descriptions of reading and writing, which is why I include it in full:

> Assuming that we agree with composition scholars, rhetoricians, linguists, philosophers, literacy scholars, and others that writing is a process of learning, that it is about making meaning rather than spitting out a series of facts and figures, that it is about analyzing, integrating, and understanding historical, political, and social context in which we are located, then we need to challenge machine scoring on these counts. Machine-scoring machines "see" texts as isolated artifacts. These machines cannot understand texts as social instruments, as organic entities that work to help writers and readers make sense of social and political environments. (p. 37)

We can and should challenge claims to the contrary, though we need to do so with the full understanding that writing assessments moved in this direction throughout the 20th century. Machine-scored writing is not an isolated incident that is an exception to the rule.

We also need to understand that some of the ways we in the field have promoted the assessment of writing has directly contributed to the current situation in which we are now embroiled. Pointing our fingers at "them" (whoever "they" may be) might be satisfying on one level, but it does not address our culpability or do anything to promote systematic reform, which needs to happen at every level of responsibility within the assessment system. Any revolution of writing assessment should begin by acknowledging ways in which we own or have abdicated responsibility in the current system.

WRITING EXPERTS' EXPERIENCES WITH MACHINE-SCORED WRITING

Among the most enlightening branches of scholarship on machine-scored writing are the accounts from writing experts who have been given the opportunity to test machine-scoring systems outside the strict controls of the companies that developed them. While we as outsiders to the company can never know definitively what machines are actually counting — the algorithms are proprietary to the companies who develop them, and it is not in their interest to reveal their formulas and thus admit how reductive the measurements are — we get a glimpse into the machines' inner workings in the narratives provided by Anne Herrington and Charles Moran, Tim McGee, and Edmund Jones, among others. Their experiences relate directly to the rhetorical nature of writing and ways writers understand their audiences and shape their discourse to respond to their perceived needs. Without the prospect of the human audience, the rhetorical situation of the writing task becomes hollow, a game in which the writer attempts, not to communicate anything meaningful to a reader, but rather to write to "psych out" a machine in order to manipulate and attain a desired score. That is not a direction we should pursue or the test toward which we as writing teachers want to teach.

In Herrington and Moran's experience with machine scoring (2001), Herrington writes a series of drafts for WritePlacer Plus in an attempt to determine the rating criteria of the technology. Her first draft, which she purposefully ends 50 words short of the recommended length and without a neat conclusion, receives a 3 on a scale of 1–6. After lengthening the essay by the required amount of words and adding a positive conclusion, she is "rewarded" with a rating of 5. Finally, she changes the concluding paragraph so that it is sarcastic, but the essay still receives a rating of 5 (pp. 488–489). From those experiences, Herrington and Moran suggest that the machine rates essay length most highly and penalizes for nontraditional mechanical conventions (p. 490). Since her changes were relatively controlled (word length, conclusions, etc.) and the score was raised two full points, they have good reason to believe that these factors play a significant role in the score she receives. More important, though, they note the distinct absence of human reaction to her revised version, in which she adds a bit of sarcasm. The lack of human response is a significant shift for those who write in authentic contexts and have grown accustomed to imagining their audience.

In one of the most memorable texts I read as part of my preparation to teach college writing, Mem Fox (1988) in "Notes from the Battlefield: Towards a Theory of Why People Write" explores the motivation of humans to engage in writing. Her conclusion is that people write because it matters, they write because they care about something, they write for response, and they write for relationships (p. 112). Part of what matters most, she concludes, is the human response writers receive to their writing; she relates an example, not laughing hard enough at something her daughter wrote for her. What responses do computers have to a piece of writing? None. What relationships are formed between the writer and the reader when the reader is a computer? None. The only thing that is produced is a score and perhaps some canned responses that are likely as vague and ambiguous as a daily horoscope. As educators who care about the success of our students and how writing is represented to them, we cannot promote such shallow responses to student writing. Computerized essay scoring lacks rhetorical understanding, human interaction, response, and emotion, fundamentally changing the writing situation. While psychometricians cite subjective reading and emotion as a weakness in writing assessment systems, human response may actually be one of the most important factors for a writer writing an authentic text.

In another narrative of an educator's testing the technology, Tim McGee (2006) recounts his experiences with Intelligent Essay Assessor (IEA), a program that claims to measure meaning. After writing a series of essays that were scored by IEA, he conducts a series of three simple experiments to see if he can confirm the claim that the computer can read and score for meaningful content. In his first experiment, he reverses the order of sentences on a biology essay, resulting in no change to the score. In a second experiment, McGee changes the facts of his initial essay so that all the factual material will be incorrect, which also results in no change to the initial score. Clearly, this program cannot search for, identify, or "measure factual content" as its marketing materials claim. In his final experiment, McGee revises an essay in such a way that it is complete nonsense. Finally, the score is lowered, but only by one point in one area. In fact, it receives a higher score on another area and thus the final score remains the same. McGee notes that since he has published the results of his threefold experiment in national venues the company has "toned down" its claims about reading for meaning and content in its more recent marketing materials.

Edmund Jones (2006) of Seton Hall, suspecting that the machine valued the length of the text disproportionately, tested the ACCUPLACER essay-scoring software by copying and pasting two opposing essays together that had each originally scored 7s. The result was as he expected. The longer text, regardless of the contradictory content, scored a 10 (p. 101). He also pasted two essays on completely different subjects together, which raised the score to a 9, confirming that in fact essay length must be a considerable criterion in the scoring algorithm for this software package (p. 101). In addition to essay length, Jones tested the "correctness" feature of the scoring, something that would conceivably be easier for a machine to do well, by taking an error-ridden student essay and correcting the surface-level mistakes. This experiment resulted in increasing the score from a 6 to an 8, which shows that the program is indeed able to count surface-level aspects of correctness (p. 103). Even though he eventually concludes that the machine favors/penalizes certain kinds of errors over others—the machine responds more to misspellings and "obvious grammatical errors" more than to subtle word choice and syntax problems that often convey more meaning in the essay (p. 105)—he was not able to produce with certainty a more comprehensive list of what matters most to the machine, only that certain surface-level features "counted" more than others, quite literally in this case.

This discussion reminds me of Larry Beason's (2001) article in *College Composition and Communication*, in which he describes readers ranking errors along a continuum to determine which are most bothersome. While the subjects have little difficulty identifying their level of distress, the study found little to no agreement on which errors are most annoying (p. 45). That very well could be true of scoring software as well. We might acknowledge that errors are a problem and will be penalized, but we cannot know what each program constitutes as error, how errors are identified by the machine, and ultimately how much students are penalized for different types of error. This confirms Bob Broad's (2003) suggestion that criteria in the way of measurable outcomes will be a site for future battles in computer-scored writing: "Therefore the area of future struggle will be over which outcomes (that is, which kinds of learning, skill, and knowledge) are valued most highly" (p. 231). He suggests that writing experts will continue to highlight the more complex and nuanced skills, knowledge, and relationships in writing while testing will continue to promote reductive, isolable elements of writing that can be identified and quantified by the machine.

Unless the companies allow us unprecedented access, we will never know exactly how computers score human writing. We can be sure that what the machines are counting is becoming more complex, and I have no doubt that they are able to score quickly and consistently. But I will continue to resist the idea that they are "reading" texts in a meaningful way. The technicians who develop and market the technology are doing a better job making it appear that the machines are reading—having the program "comment" or provide rationale for scores that mimic human readers—but imitation in this case is not sufficient. In fact, making it appear as if the machine is reading may actually be more damaging in the end, since it may influence how the public understands reading in the first place as it applies to writing assessments. Even if the definition of reading were opened to the algorithmic calculation, machine scoring undermines the rhetorical situation, substituting an audience that the reader should analyze and anticipate with an inanimate scoring mechanism. This considerable difference undercuts the ways we understand and teach writing and threatens the more valid and ethical methods of assessing writing that are being done at the local level, which would never be able to compete with the cost efficiency of this mechanized process. This is a battle that we cannot afford to lose.

THE MISDIRECTION OF MECHANIZATION

In the discussion of machine scoring and other mechanized writing assessments, somewhere along the way we have lost the idea of how and why people read and write within meaningful rhetorical situations. We have abandoned what we know to be true about writing for the promise of a cheap, mechanized solution to a problem that we have not had opportunity to help define or address. A machine reading and scoring a student text is devoid of rhetorical context, which profoundly changes the situation in which writers appeal to their perceived audience. This rhetorical knowledge and sophistication is one of the core criteria for effective writing. According to Lloyd Bitzer (1968), a rhetorical situation includes (1) the exigence or the problem which initiates or compels the communication that is convoluted in mechanized writing assessments), (2) the audience (which is anywhere from unknown to nonexistent in mechanized writing assessments), and (3) the constraints (which in this case are many, especially since the writer has no clear idea of how the scorer or the machine will judge his or her writing). In the case of mechanized writing assessment, the exigence is cloudy, beyond the need to produce a certain score in order to gain access to educational opportunities, and the audience is erased, leaving the writer to have to guess what a machine might be able to count as good writing. This is simply not acceptable for assessments upon which many important educational decisions are made. A rhetorical situation with testing as the exigence, no human audience, and heavy with constraints is not anything like authentic assessment, which is the goal of contemporary writing assessment and should not be sacrificed in favor of mechanistic assessment solutions.

Beyond machine scoring, we need to challenge the trend toward mechanized writing assessments with technologies. As we complicate the dominant cultural assumptions and narratives that technologies are superior to humans in educational and assessment, we can point toward the ways in which mechanized assessments contain as much bias as an human reader and that the values of speed and consistency may not be as important in the long run as the ability to read for content, context, meaning, and understanding. Although machine-scored student writing is the most blatant, aggressive, and potentially harmful manifestation of mechanization in writing assessment, it did not suddenly appear out of nowhere. Writing assessment has been steadily progressing in this direction through increasingly mechanized processes and procedures, even some that we in the discipline have supported. In one way of thinking, machine-scored writing is the most logical progression of writing assessment with technology, since it has evolved within a culture of positivism and desired efficiency. A, if not *the*, primary reason we are at a place now where student writing is being assessed by computers for high-stakes educational decisions is less about the constituent computer technologies that are currently available and more about a mindset in educational assessment that elevates mechanization over human reading and decision making.

I have no doubt that testing companies that are scoring direct writing assessments with human readers will move to embrace computerized scoring in the near future. While they had to respond to the outcry for direct measures of student writing, the cultural and economic forces are currently in place to shift from human to machine-scored writing. This coupled with the increasingly tight budgets at institutions—which may previously have invested in better assessment measures—will push us with the rhetoric of crisis to adopt mechanized assessments that transfer the burden of cost to students and will be defended on the basis of their efficiency and reliability and will become a substitute for human reading. It is this kind of mindset within the context of writing assessments with technologies that we must be aware of and vigilant against, even if these assessments are not at our particular institutions. Once such assessments gain a foothold in institutions across the nation, it will be easier for them to convince other institutions to compromise in similar ways. While writing assessments with technologies hold enormous promise—as I will outline in the next chapter—we must work against the ways in which technologies propel us toward the mechanization and dehumanization of writing assessment.

Hyperactive Hypertechs

A lot of people my age out there are so hyper. I like hyper people.
   —Edward Furlong (teen actor in *Terminator 2* and *American History X*)

THE TEXTS AND TECHNOLOGIES (techs) students are writing and using to write move beyond the print texts of the 20th century. They are creating what I will call "hyperactive hypertechs"—my play on the prefix *hyper*, which, according to the *Oxford English Dictionary* (http://dictionary.oed. com/), denotes excess, extravagance, going above and beyond the ordinary degree, or passing or surpassing all measure. Hypertechs and digital texts are dynamic, multimodal, interactive, and connected. They can be produced, reproduced, written, and rewritten with relative ease and flexibility and distributed more broadly than ever before almost instantly. While *hyperactivity* in this chapter denotes action surrounding writing and related literacy events, I am well aware as the father of three young children, that the term also connotes a type of highly energetic behavior often ascribed to youth, which I find particularly tantalizing when thinking about the types of writing being composed with digital technologies. Channeling the ideas of excess and abundance with a sense of unbridled energy, we have the texts and techs of the digital age: hypertechs.

While a portion of writing teachers find these new texts and techs compelling and exciting, others are wary, fearing that we may not be able to adjust to or manage 21st-century literacies. While most writing teachers understood the value of incorporating early digital technologies such as word processing into the classroom, some of the newer digital technologies many be less apparently connection to our pedagogy and curriculum: wikis, blogs, digital video, social networking (e.g., MySpace, Facebook, and Twitter) and social bookmarking (e.g., del.icio.us and Diigo), and the expanding range of audio/visual technologies (e.g., Flickr, YouTube, Wordle, Prezi, and Vuvox). One argument for including digital technologies such as these in the writing classes of the 21st century is that students' authentic composing outside school most often happens in such spaces and includes more than linguistic texts. Students find exigencies and authentic audiences in these spaces. They can be political, personal, or practical. Other times they are playful, artistic, or irreverent. Most often they are a hybrid of different types of communication, but, important for our purposes, they are the types of composing that are furthest from being captured and measured by mechanistic writing assessments. While standardized assessments are still grappling with dilemmas of strictly controlling word processing, students—and many writing classes—are decades beyond this point.

As a writing teacher who focuses on the rhetorical nature of texts and situations, I find the opportunities of digital texts and techs appealing—even in their instability, hybridity, and experimentality—though the inner assessor and former program director cringes at the thought of the problems these new techs and texts pose as I venture in this direction. Composing in and with hypertechs offers me a sense of excitement and even risk as a writer and a teacher of writing. Not knowing how my students will respond to unusual assignments, a greater range of available strategies, and often unknown constraints keeps me engaged as a teacher and more fully focused on the goals on my courses. It is much harder for me to shift into autopilot when teaching digital techs and texts.

While these are the benefits I see for myself and others as teachers of writing, I engage with digital texts and techs not for me but for the students in my classes. While writing will doubtlessly evolve in their lifetimes, students know these spaces, have reasons to write in them, and would benefit from a more critical examination of how they interact in them. That is not to say that this is the only type of writing my students complete, but it becomes an important point of intersection between school-based literacies and those in which they engage outside of school, which is becoming an increasingly important connection to teachers of writing (Brant, 2001; Houle, Kimball, & McKee, 2005; Moss, 1994; Selber, 2004; Stroupe, 2007; Yancey, 2004a).

As a case in point, several years ago I asked students in one of my classes to reflect on their personal writing habits and assumptions. Most defined writing in fairly traditional ways and most noted that they do not write often outside school. Later in the semester, however, quite by accident I ran across one of my student's blogs. He wrote often. He wrote with authority. People responded to his writing. Going back into my files and finding his initial reflections, though, I found that he was one of the many who claimed not to write very often. Seeing the obvious disjuncture between his response and what I had stumbled upon, I asked him about it after class one day. He responded quite matter-of-factly that, since I was an English teacher, he did not think I would classify his blogging as "real writing." I am reminded here of both David Bartholmae's (1996) critique of "the institutional desire to organize and evaluate the writing of *unauthorized writers*, to control writing in practice, and to define it as an object of professional scrutiny" (p. 11; emphasis mine) as well as Paul Kameen's (2000) distinction that students need more than just to be told that they are authors: "It's not enough, really, just to authorize him to speak. He needs to have something that he genuinely wants to say, and he needs to be able to enter the conversation with the prospect of actually being heard" (p. 162). In the blogosphere, this student was an author in ways he never considered himself to be within a classroom space. While I thought he was one of the better writers in the class and attributed at least some of that to his extracurricular writing interests, more important, he saw a disconnect between writing in and out of school in ways that are not helpful to him or for us as educators.

Not only do I see the writing students do outside class as valid, I am increasingly concerned about what happens to composition when we delegitimize or marginalize the writing students do outside class, even those done in digital spaces that do not look much like writing students have traditionally done in the academy. While English teachers have a long history of blaming unsanctioned student writing for the degeneration of their literacy skills (e.g., e-mail, instant messaging, texting, tweeting), we need to use these opportunities as teachable moments to talk about how and why language evolves, differing expectations of audiences, and how technologies shape the forms and our understanding of communication. Thus, while hypertechs include a broad array of activities, artifacts, and processes in digital spaces, I will focus on three aspects that I believe relate directly to writing and its assessment for educational decision making: hypertexts, hypermedia, and hyperattention. In each case, I will explore how the technology is (re)shaping communication through texts and how we can and should respond via writing assessments with technologies.

HYPERTEXT: CONNECTIVITY ARTICULATED

According to George Landow (1997), *hypertext* is defined broadly as "an information medium that links verbal and nonverbal information" (p. 3), to which Craig Stroupe (2007) responds that Landow makes a misstep in not distinguishing between hypertext and hypermedia, lumping them together and privileging the former (p. 607). Like Stroupe, I think a distinction between hypertext and hypermedia is valuable, not so much because one overshadows the other, but because I see them as serving two distinct rhetorical functions for writers and thus affecting the context and criteria for writing assessment. Even though *hypertext* can describe a wide array of digital texts, it is most often understood in terms of its connectivity. Linked texts, especially those that result in a non- or multilinear arrangement, provide a rhetorical nuance for writers, since they have to anticipate multiple paths via which a reader might navigate the text. While it is worth noting that readers do not necessarily progress through print texts from beginning to end, hypertext invites multiple paths and options often in more obvious ways. Moreover, a writer of a print text might be more justified to claim that readers are responsible for information they present earlier in the text, since the assumption, though false, is that print texts are to be read from beginning to end.

For example, if I choose to skip to the end of a book to read the conclusion, I should not be surprised or frustrated to find that there might be items included there that I do not fully understand. I would not criticize the author because my way of navigating the text caused me to struggle in comprehending it. However, if I were to read a hypertext that required me to navigate the text in one particular way in order to understand the ideas, I could more reasonably argue that the text should allow for multiple progressions through the text. It is this type of difference, I believe, that compels digital publications like those we find in *Kairos: A Journal of Rhetoric, Technology, and Pedagogy* to ask for texts that are designed for the screen rather than those made for print that simply get cut into smaller pieces and linked. It is relatively easy for a reader to distinguish between texts designed for linear or nonlinear navigation. That's not to say that linear texts on the screen do not serve an important purpose, but we should not conflate them with hypertexts that invite and expect multiple navigation paths. Despite what may be a move in the field away from hypertext writing and claims by such notable scholars as Jay David Bolter (2008)—who argues that while hypertext was initially avant-garde and poststructuralist, the World Wide Web, betrayed its potential by simply reproducing print online instead of creating sustainable, new types of tests. Hypertexts still provide interesting insights into student writing for the purposes of assessment. How and why writers make the connections between and among their texts, their goals, their education, their professions, and their lives that we see in electronic portfolios (ePortfolios) can be worthwhile for students and provide valuable data for teachers of writing.

When print portfolios were introduced to composition studies, they were most often theorized with links to process (Belanoff & Dickson, 1991; Black, Helton, & Sommers, 1994; Hamp-Lyon & Condon, 1993; Yancey, 1992), multiple literacies and genres (Belanoff, 1994), diversity (Broad, 1994), authentic writing and assessment (Black et al., 1994), and reflection and self-assessment (Yancey, 1996a, 1996b, 1998). In portfolios students compile multiple texts—from formal to informal, from drafts to revised and edited works depending on how they are defined—in order to demonstrate more about students' knowledge and skill than a single piece of writing or a final product could communicate. This meshed neatly at the time with process pedagogies that emphasized stages in writing, multiple drafts, revision, writing as learning, and multiple contexts for writing.

My initial decision to use classroom-based print portfolios for teaching and writing assessment seemed simple enough. I was all about process; I liked to see the progression of drafts, feedback, and revisions that students completed for each assignment. And most of all, I liked that I could delay the assignment of grades for student writing until the end of the term, giving students the maximum opportunity, within the limited time provided by the university, to work on their writing and reflect on themselves as writers before I would step in and evaluate. From my perspective, the best pedagogies, teachers, and programs in the country were using portfolios, so they were widely accepted, and I did not have to convince many program directors of why I wanted to use them. In fact I remember saying—naively, but with a certain amount of conviction nonetheless—that if a writing teacher graded each paper and collected them all at the end of the term, it should be called something other than a "portfolio." Perhaps it should be called "a bunch of papers in a folder," because portfolio assessment required looking at the body of student work holistically; it was not an additive evaluation of each individual essay. According to Yancey (2001), portfolios needed to be a collection, selection, and reflection as well as a methodology or process for providing evaluation.

Since the introduction of portfolios to the teaching and assessment of writing, we have seen an ever-increasing range of possibilities they provide and need to adopt a more flexible understanding of them. We need to distinguish between our understanding of portfolio assessment and portfolios as an artifact or space to collect, select, and reflect on multiple texts. From process to showcase portfolios, from teaching to student writing portfolios, from classroom to large-scale assessment portfolios, we can no longer assume that the term "portfolio" has a specific context, shape, meaning, or function in our classes or institutions. Historically, though, portfolios and their assessment became a type of educational fix-all (Callahan, 1995; Murphy & Grant, 1996). Callahan (1995) pokes fun at the way that portfolios were prescribed for any educational ailment: "Apathetic students? Try portfolios. Students obsessed with grades? Use portfolios. Inconsistent departmental grading practices? Require portfolios. Culturally biased tests? Replace them with portfolios. Want to stimulate creativity? Process instruction? Reflective teaching and learning? Portfolios, portfolios, portfolios (p. 118). Perhaps the biggest change I've seen, however, is the shift from paper to ePortfolios. Not only can I now fit all my student portfolios for the semester on a single jump drive, but portfolio assessment is again emerging on the scene of classroom and large-scale assessment similarly to the way it did years ago. Much of the work around ePortfolios is found in institutional assessments, writing in the disciplines, or writing across the curriculum programs.

What constitutes an ePortfolio? And where is the line that if crossed would lead me to make the argument that it really isn't an ePortfolio—it's more like an electronic database? I believe that the primary distinguishing features of ePortfolios lie in their connectivity and reflection, specifically what is communicated by authors through the connections they make and how the reflective texts they connect to represent what they are learning. Yancey (2001) answers the question of how portfolios change when they become electronic: "In some ways, nothing changes; yet changes in key features—especially the addition of linking—seem to make the electronic portfolio a different kind of portfolio altogether, a difference almost in kind rather than degree" (p. 20).

"A difference almost in kind rather than degree." That is a provocative claim, but it represents an elusive component of this reemerging writing assessment technology. For connections to occur, there need to be multiple texts, though in writing it is rarely as simple as two separate items that have a definable relationship with one another. Connections in ePortfolios can be between different artifacts, between a writer's goals and his or her current abilities, between course outcomes and student performance, between reflections and essays or process, between feedback and revision. The list goes on. Connections are the key, and hypertext provides a means—though not exclusively—to represent those relationships. So before we pronounce hypertext dead in composition classes, we should reexamine the value of hypertext in ePortfolio assessment as well as ways we can teach students about writing and self-representation via this hypertech.

What we see now is that portfolios have largely evolved into ePortfolios and have become more flexible and inclusive (Yancey, 2004b) with the amount of storage and the increasing range of student work that can be digitized and included as artifacts to represent student work. In other words, ePortfolios are often more than merely three to four essays produced in 1st-year composition class with a reflective cover letter, something that might have been more the norm in the print heyday of portfolios. Yes, ePortoflios include essays, but they also contain other genres of writing: spreadsheets, designs, research posters, coding, audio files, photos, video, external links, and nearly any other student-produced artifact that can be captured digitally. Yancey (2001), in describing classroom ePortfolios, shows why they have evolved to include a wider range of possibilities: "Classroom portfolios can vary considerably, especially when we think about them along four parameters or dimensions: (1) type and level of class . . . ; (2) purpose of the portfolio; (3) audience for the portfolio; and (4) criteria for assessment. Regardless of the diversity of portfolio models, however, they all make the same request: that students assume responsibility for documenting and interpreting their own learning" (p. 17). ePortfolios have the potential to bridge values in the discipline and digital environments in ways that provide a different perspective than that of efficiency and objectivity, often associated with digital technologies, as represented in the two examples that follow.

A Tale of Two ePortfolio Initiatives

To show a range of motives, practices, and assessments connected with ePortfolios, I will provide two brief examples of institutional ePortfolios. While these are only two instances, they could hardly be more dissimilar and as such show why ePortfolios cannot be a generic answer to opportunities and problems of assessing student writing. While it has enormous potential, ePortfolio assessment requires resources—writing expertise, careful consideration of how assessments will be implemented, and a commitment of time and financial resources—to ensure that the assessment will provide students the feedback they need to improve as writers while providing educators with the information they need to make accurate and appropriate decisions about students, teachers, programs, and institutions.

The first example is an extension of a narrative I provided in the previous chapter when I was the director of 1st-year composition (FYC). I partnered with my dean of undergraduate studies on an institutional ePortfolio initiative. One of my first decisions was to reintroduce ePortfolios into the FYC curriculum. As the program reeled from university-wide budget cuts, it took a defensive position, jettisoning its work with digital texts and ePortfolios. A top priority for me as a new composition director—and I knew it would be a visibly ideological statement—was to define work with digital texts and ePortfolios as central to the teaching of composition. As evidence of the visibility of the programmatic ePortfolio, within a few months of introducing it, I was summoned to the office of the dean of undergraduate studies and asked to partner with the university's general education ePortfolio. While it was clear to me that the dean had the interests of the students in mind, it also became clear that there were others who were more interested in data mining, collecting information about students to use for the looming external accreditation. So the battleground was set, and several questions emerged that became the basis of our ensuing negotiation:

1. Who would design, define, and assign the ePortfolio?
2. Who would determine the content of the ePortfolio and the criteria for the assessment?
3. Who would read the ePortfolios? For what purpose and to what consequence? What feedback/instruction would students receive? How would the results be used at the institution? What would happen to students who did not successfully complete the ePortfolio?
4. Would students be asked to reflect on their work or make connections in the ePortfolio, or would it simply be a collection of their work (an electronic database to mine for institutional assessment purposes)?

In answering these questions, it became clear to me over the course of the year that student learning was secondary to administrative assessment needs in this particular system. As I mentioned previously, students were required to use the university-purchased course management system to house and build their ePortfolio. In short, this system was horrendous. Plus, the predetermined design was excruciatingly boring. Students had little control over design unless they knew how to go into the coding and change it themselves, and it was merely a file uploading, drag-and-drop system. There was little compelling or engaging about it. At the time we launched the ePortfolio, no one knew who would read the portfolios or the assessment criteria or if students would get any feedback.

In terms of criteria for writing in the portfolio, a generous university citizen in the education department put together a scoring rubric on her own time, but it was as expected—systematic and mechanistic, though to her credit she was given no resources, support, or vision that would have challenged her to produce anything different. It was clear that whoever would score the ePortfolio would need to be calibrated. Students would never know the reader, nor would they receive any feedback other than a single summary judgment. Finally, there was no motivation for students built into the successful completion of the ePortfolio except suggestions of punitive action against students that surfaced from time to time, such as blocking them from registering for classes if the ePortfolio were not complete or acceptable. It was motivation by stick rather than carrot. Student learning, student needs, student support, student interests, student creativity, student investment, and student use beyond the institutional assessment was not part of the plan. One could argue that students, even though it was their writing, were tangential to the assessment from the beginning.

The most distressing thing to me is that students were not asked to reflect upon or make any connections between and among their artifacts, goals, competencies, ambitions, programs, or career goals. Students could include a reflective essay if they so chose, but it was not part of the instructions, process, or evaluation framework. In my mind, therefore, this was not really a portfolio assessment but simply a digital database with links to student artifacts. In partnering with this initiative, I failed the program— certainly the teachers, but, more important, the students. Fortunately, as so many teachers and students have done for years, some worked outside the constraints of a limited and limiting system and developed thoughtful, engaged texts. Even flawed assessments are not always enough to suppress the energy and creativity of the best students and teachers. I know, however, that for every positive experience I could identify, there were far more negative ones that people had with this particular ePortfolio model. For the record, I should note that this system did not last long at the institution. In fact, since then they have developed a much better system that gives them the opportunity to collect data on the back end of the process rather than foregrounding it as their primary purpose.

My second narrative of a large-scale ePortfolio assessment could not be more dissimilar from the first, demonstrating again that it is far less about the instrument or tool and more about the context and values that drive an assessment technology. I have had the privilege over the past several years to consult on an ePortfolio program at a small private institution where the writing program was able to tap into the local context and strengths to produce an assessment technology that works on a number of levels. Well before they launched the program, this group of faculty were talking about the value of an ePortfolio assessment and considering different models in light of their own context. Their portfolio initiative was driven by shared interests between and among faculty at the institution, and student learning was paramount to their exigence. When I first visited their campus, they asked me to provide an overview of methods that could be used for a large-scale writing assessment of the portfolios and encourage faculty to think and talk about their local context. I did not come in to promote a particular system or solution, nor was there a sense of top-down administrative pressure to initiate such an assessment.

Because of the local context, this particular model started as a paper portfolio assessment that would, over a 4- to 5-year span, transition to ePortfolios. While all 1st-year students would submit a portfolio at the end of the year, it was a small enough population that a group of invested, interdisciplinary faculty could assess them over the course of a week at the beginning of the summer. This group of interdisciplinary faculty took ownership of the assessment from the outset, deciding, for example, that they wanted at least one piece of writing to be included in the portfolio that was not written in class, to determine how students could respond to a writing prompt without the support structure of a class and teacher. They also determined the criteria and language for the evaluation. Modeling Bob Broad's dynamic criteria mapping methodology from *What We Really Value* (2003), which values teacher expertise and local knowledge, we examined portfolio models from several institutions and, predictably, found that the faculty had different ideas of what they wanted from the assessment and how they defined successful student writing.

Articulating, discussing, and negotiating writing are among the best moments in the process of implementing locally controlled writing assessments. Together and through discussion and compromise, we developed a framework to assess student writing that reflected the values of the faculty and considered the needs of students, providing buy-in at two important levels that are often ignored in large-scale assessment models. The system was designed to be flexible enough to evolve, each year revisiting the criteria and considering the students' needs and goals. We modified the scoring guide for the subsequent year, making adjustments based on how the faculty readers perceived what the guide communicates well, what limitations they felt in using it, and how students received and understood the feedback they received the past year. This large-scale writing assessment provides more than a score or a simple pass/fair framework; it provides descriptive formative feedback to the students so they can develop as writers.

One might say that this particular writing assessment was "locally owned and operated," which makes a difference to the students and faculty alike. Like William Smith's model (Smith, 1993), mentioned earlier, readers make decisions about students instead of merely assigning a score to a text. Not only do students receive holistic assessments (either pass or resubmit); each receives at least two scoring guides with descriptive feedback on writing criteria marked and annotated by faculty readers. In the assessment process, "disagreements" between readers are not understood as errors; time is allotted at the end of each day when readers meet in groups and talk about portfolios with a split score, providing faculty development throughout the week. As part of the feedback loop, a list of workshops offered by the writing center appears at the bottom of the form that readers can check by way of recommendation for further support. At no time in this process are readers required to suppress their experience or expertise, nor is the decision about students made based on the assessment downplayed to encourage mechanistic scoring. Students' successes and needs are central to the design and implementation of this assessment.

Finally, students are prompted to reflect and make connections in their portfolio. One of the required texts in the ePortfolio is a critical reflection piece that provides a rationale for the selection of each artifact; what students are learning about themselves as writers and thinkers; self-assessment; and applications to future writing contexts, such as other coursework, their majors, and their future professional settings. These reflective prompts invite students to make and see connections between and among many components of their writing, educational, and professional skills and goals. The reflective text is such a critical component of the assessment that the faculty readers have developed a separate section on the student feedback sheet specifically for it.

Assessing Hypertexts

If we want electronic portfolios and other hypertext writing to be student-based rather than assessment-based, we can achieve that end through the way we develop, define, and implement our writing assessments. Only a small portion of students will explicitly see and make sense of connections between what we are doing in writing classes and other contexts unless they are provided with a kind of scaffolding to get there, which is where the work on reflection becomes most helpful. Jody Murray (2009), by equating reflection with self-assessment, suggests that reflection does not live up to its promise:

> Often touted as the panacea of assessment, self-assessment may not be as useful as some writing teachers might think, especially in terms of helping students to see the potential in the writing they do while, simultaneously, helping them to value the dynamic nature of most multimodal writing in new media today. Though reflection is for the most part a valuable exercise, it must be combined with a rigorous method of self-assessment that connects the process elements with the end product in such a way as to discourage any notions of rigidity or finality. (p. 186)

While I agree with Murray that reflective texts should be read rhetorically, I have found in my own work with students that asking them for evaluative judgments of their own work is conflicting, so instead of asking them to evaluate their work via reflections, I have been asking them for the rhetorical rationale for the decisions they made as writers, especially when dealing with hypertexts and other forms of hypermedia.

So 10 years ago my reflective prompts for students tended to be self-evaluations, much in the way Murray describes: What do you like best about this piece of writing? What are you least pleased with as the author of this piece? How well do you think you used sources for this piece of writing? What is your favorite portion? Now my prompts for reflections look different and most often begin with *why*: Why did you narrow your topic the way you did in light of your other alternatives? Why did you include the visuals you did for this piece? Why did you design your navigation the way you did? Why did you include each piece of writing in this portfolio? The *why* questions suggest to students that the choices they make should have a reason that can be articulated within a larger vision for the project, whatever it may be. I find this type of reflection to be more useful with high-tech writing than pure self-assessment.

The scholarship of reflection, regardless of its emphasis or type, is quite clear; students need to be guided to reflection at multiple points during the process to maximize its effectiveness (Smith & Yancey, 2000). While this can happen in different ways, I tend to provide a series of reflective questions, like those above, at different points in the writing process. These focus students' attention on the rhetorical elements we have been emphasizing at the time. The reflections are regular and provide immediate feedback on the topic at hand, but, more important, they provide a systematic record of students' rhetorical strategies for them to consider as they make connections in their final portfolios. If I do not create the space and exigence for consistent reflections during the term, I do not expect that my students can go back and recapture their thinking from earlier moments in the term. Consider the following four examples of student reflections upon completing an assignment that students can use at the end of the semester to make connections in an ePortfolio:

Emani:
I think I underestimated how powerful imagery can be. I wasn't entirely sure how I was going to go about putting visuals into this kind of project in the very beginning. I thought, due to the nature of my subject, it would mostly be copies of Bruce's artwork and perhaps some other artwork of his contemporaries. What I realized, however, was that using the pictures effectively meant I could get my text across in a much clearer way. I decided to let the visuals and the text form the base of the narrative instead of just having pictures sitting there.

Jonathan:
In this project I tried to maintain a fine balance between written visuals, visuals with video, and audio because I didn't want this project to seem like a PowerPoint; however, I also didn't want it to

turn out looking like a pure feature-documentary. By using different types of sources and choosing which elements to include in the
project, I was able to extract and include information I felt was most
informative as well as appealing to an audience unaware of the
struggles of the Beninese people. Overall, the visuals played a significant role in the project, specifically with regards to the children
of Benin who have endured lasting and obvious pain.

Ashley:
As I did with each part of the entire assignment, I visualized in my
head the pictures I wanted to use to convey what I was trying to
get across to the audience. Adding some of those pictures became
problematic at first, because I was not allowed to take pictures of the
children in the program, and I had to use what Jumpstart provided
for me. However, using their pictures, video, and clips from the
Internet, I think I was able to provide a clear sense for my story of
how the Jumpstart program works. Overlapping some of the pictures with my audio was troubling at times because I felt like I was
repeating the same image over and over again by just showing the
kids, or the volunteers working with the kids; but in the end I think
I was able to mix things up a bit by adding in a few short video clips
of the kid's opinions about the program.

Shane:
At first I thought it'd be easy to compose audio for a podcast, con-
dense the material a bit and then write a script. Sounds easy but
what ended up happening was that when I began reading the script
aloud I noticed how artificial it sounded, despite the written component being perfectly sound. I began to notice how the way the sentences are constructed and the words you use vary greatly between
written style and speaking style. So as a composer I attempted to
modify my words to sound more colloquial without sacrificing the
academic flavor of presenting the information.

Guiding students to rhetorical reflections at regular intervals can provide
a base for them to construct larger reflective texts and connections in a
course portfolio. If students do not have these touch points in writing, it
becomes far more difficult for them to construct their thinking and learning over longer periods of time such as a semester.

In addition to providing a chronology of thinking and learning for
students, reflection can be an important point of assessment for teachers of
writing. Critics of reflection point to an inability to determine authenticity

of voice in reflection or the appropriateness of using this type of personal writing to evaluate students' performances. Murray (2009), though skeptical of reflective self-assessment, as seen in the section above, notes that it can be successful if the reflective writing is understood as rhetorical. He encourages teachers to compare student writing with the reflective writing to resolve any "disparity" they see between the texts (p. 187). Similarly, I find claims students make in their reflections as something that requires textual evidence. If I have done my job well as a writing teacher, the students should be able to understand that concept.

Reflections and the claim within them are only as meaningful as the textual evidence that accompany them. It is the relationship between them that becomes the meaningful place to evaluate student performance. Claims with no evidence demonstrates either a lack of self-awareness on the part of a writer or that the writer is trying to claim something that he or she has not actually accomplished, or what Wesier calls "schmoozing" if it is accompanied by thinly veiled flattery (qtd. in Reynolds, 2000).

Equally problematic, however, is evidence of solid work without the student's making any claims about it. Again, this shows either a lack of self-awareness or that the writing skills remain tacit in an environment in which part of demonstrated learning means students becoming aware as writers. Effective reflection demonstrates a balance between claims and evidence that are mutually reinforcing. The claims are made tangible and meaningful in looking at the evidence, and the evidence provides insights into the writer's claims about him- or herself. Reflection helps both students and teachers articulate and assess if those connections are being made. The hypertext technologies of electronic portfolios provide a platform to link and communicate the connections they are making within this framework.

In addition to encouraging reflective connectivity via questions throughout the semester, it is important to make sure that the requirement exists in the assignment description and in the assessment mechanization. Take, for example, the following descriptors, found in scoring guides published online:

IUPUI, Office of Service Learning
(ctl.iupui.edu/common/uploads/library/CSL/CSL529447.doc)
Reflective Practitioner:

- *Clarity.* The language is clear and expressive. The reader can create a mental picture of the situation being described. Abstract concepts are explained accurately. Explanation of concepts makes sense to an uninformed reader.

- *Relevance.* The learning experience being reflected upon is relevant and meaningful to student and course learning goals.
- *Analysis*: The reflection moves beyond simple description of the experience to an analysis of how the experience contributed to student understanding of self, others, and/or course concepts.
- *Interconnections.* The reflection demonstrates connections between the experience and material from other courses; past experience; and/or personal goals.
- *Self-criticism.* The reflection demonstrates ability of the students to question their own biases, stereotypes, preconceptions, and/or assumptions and define new modes of thinking as a result.

Central Piedmont Community College
(http://www.cpcc.edu/learningcollege/learning-outcomes/rubrics/
reflection_rubric.doc)
Superior Depth of Reflection:

- Response demonstrates an in-depth reflection on, and personalization of, the theories, concepts, and/or strategies presented in the course materials to date. Viewpoints and interpretations are insightful and well supported. Clear, detailed examples are provided, as applicable.

NCTE Read, Write, Think
(www.readwritethink.org)
Depth of Reflection:

- Demonstrate a conscious and thorough understanding of the writing prompt and the subject matter. This reflection can be used as an example for other students.

The point here is less about the specific ways in which effective reflection is described—in fact, reflection has any number of implications and meanings within different contexts—but more about its being defined in ways that guide students toward the type of work they are being asked to do and its providing a framework that lets them and the assessors know how it will be evaluated.

If we think the connections students make in ePortfolios are important to their learning and development as writers and thinkers, we need to make sure a framework exists within the systems to guide them through the process of self-assessment and of articulating connections through reflection and hypertext. While not a substantive component in the content of student writing, hypertext can allow students to represent the connections they see in their work. Far from being dead, hypertext in writing assessment can help students communicate what they are learning to themselves and to an audience of educators as well as show how they view their work within larger contexts. Writing assessments and technologies that allow for that work are an important part of the digital (r)evolution of writing assessment.

HYPERMEDIA

Hypermedia is the second of three hypertech evolutions that are changing the relationships between writing and its assessment. While scholars have other names for what I will call *hypermedia* in this chapter (among these names are *new media, multimedia composition, multimodal composition, digital writing,* and *electronic texts*), their commonality—though there are slight differences—is that they combine more than one media or communication modality in digital platforms. As demonstrated in Figure 5.1, what Lev Manovich (2001) calls "types of media" is closely mirrored by the New London Group's (1996) communication modes.

The classification systems are clearly parallel, though the New London Group adds gestural and multimodal communication to its list. While the gestural doesn't have an equivalent in Manovich's scheme, *multimodal* denotes combining the list, which could be done with either scheme. I am of the same mind as the New London Group, which includes *multimodal* as a separate category, since the new combined text becomes something greater than the sum of its parts, or at least substantially distinct from an additive approach. *Multimodal* thus becomes a nearly infinite category, as new texts can be produced through different groupings of textual modes. It is this difference that compels us to consider new ways to respond to

Figure 5.1. Manovich and New London Group models compared.

Manovich's Types of Media in the Computer Revolution	New London Group's Modes of Communication
1. Texts 2. Still and moving images (combined) 3. Sound 4. Spatial construction	1. Linguistic 2. Visual 3. Audio 4. Spatial 5. Gestural 6. Multimodal

and assess hypermedia in ways that go beyond simply adding new criteria or outcomes to an existing and ever expanding list.

My definition of *hypermedia* in this chapter also encompasses many ways in which composition scholars are using the term *new media* to describe certain types of texts. A notable exception is the way Anne Wysocki (2004) characterizes *new media* in relation to *media consciousness* or *awareness*:

> New media texts do not have to be digital; instead, any text that has been designed so that its materiality is not effaced can count as new media. New media texts can be made of anything . . . ; what is important is that whoever produces the text and whoever consumes it understand . . . that the various immaterialities of a text contribute to how it, like its producers and consumers, is read and understood. (p. 15)

For Wysocki a print book, a newspaper, and a handwritten letter could all be examples of new media if a certain level of conscientiousness of media affordances is met. A handwritten invitation to an event can be classified as new media as long as the reader and writer are aware, for example, of the ways the letter allows for a certain type of communication that is distinct from other media choices. Wysocki's distinction is nuanced and evocative; however, it presents significant challenges in terms of writing assessment.

For one thing, her definition requires a measurement of consciousness on the part of *both writer and reader* about the nuances, affordances, and limitations of media. While I can imagine how assessors might get this information from the writer, I am less certain about how they might elicit this from potential readers. Likewise, I am not convinced that a reader's consciousness of media should determine the classification of such texts, since that would doubtless be a slippery classification. The measure of degree of consciousness would be hard to assess. For now at least, I am engaged and challenged by Wysocki's definition of new media, but I default to a simpler definition of new media, and hypermedia, inasmuch as it pertains to writing assessment.

Although hypermedia may not yet be mainstream in educational settings, I believe it is the single most important textual revolution of the digital age and has the potential to change the ways in which writing/composing is conceptualized in and outside educational settings. We saw it in the "term wars" between writing and composing at the turn of the century. Some scholars within the discipline are committed to written texts, while others want to expand the notion of "composition" to include visuals, sound, and other hypermedia. Further complicating the distinction, however, are those who argue that "composition" is too specifically located within educational settings, especially in relationship to the general education course(s) typically delivered in the 1st year of a student's higher education. In this case, *writing* would be the more expansive term, since people in a variety of other contexts identify what they do as writing. *Composing* can be understood as either positive or negative, as it also includes a range of activities in art, music, design, engineering, and other disciplines. The arguments are varied, and I do not have a specific claim to stake in the debate. I use *writing* more than *composition* in this text because I associate composition so strongly with school-based writing, especially that in the 1st-year course that is only part of where writing is taught, and I have less trouble understanding *writing* to include multimedia.

Whether it is widely implemented or not in educational contexts, hypermedia pervades our lives and that of our students. As such, many composition and other writing classes include everything from writing Web sites to podcasts, blogs, wikis, social networking, digital video, and social bookmarking. Seemingly there is no new technology that a growing group of enthusiastic writing teachers are not willing to adopt in their writing classes. Notice how many of the applications listed above are composed of more than one type of media or modality. Even the few that appear to exist in a single medium are not necessarily limited in that way. For example, even though podcasts may be delivered exclusively as audio texts, many have written scripts or have major portions of the texts transcribed into writing.

As hypermedia is becoming more of an integral component of 21st-century literacy both in and outside the classroom, it is becoming increasingly significant in the assessment of writing. This has implications that span the continuum of theoretical and practical. According to Manovich (2001) new media texts are necessarily mathematical as well as linguistic, thus becoming programmable (p. 27). While this might not seem significant, consider the following: As I compose this book on a word processor, I see words that are meaningful. However, within the word processing program, my text is merely numbers and symbols. By virtue of this text being composed via word processor rather than pen and paper, my text can be programmed in any number of consequential ways. It could be scanned through a plagiarism detector or added to a database. It could be published to the Web and sent via attachment to a publisher halfway around the world. Let us consider what this means.

Part of what makes plagiarism-detection software marketable at this moment in time is that a majority of students are producing numerically represented texts, which allows for this type of programming of texts. A writing teacher who assigns and collects handwritten texts, for instance, does not have that same option. The reason students have unprecedented access to materials to download or copy online is because the texts are mathematical codes. These and other ramifications have come about in part because of the mathematical nature of hypermediated texts. This again shows that technology is not necessarily the problem or the solution for dilemmas in the teaching of writing. The same digitization that allows me to save, send, and edit this text also facilitates my losing it (note to self: when did I last back up my files?), having my texts appropriated or manipulated by others, or having my writing scored by a machine. This is the nature of texts and technologies at the beginning of the 21st century. Whether I approve of the consequences or not, hypermedia texts are mathematic and thus programmable. This opens texts to a number of possibilities that did not previously exist before hypermedia, which has implications for writing assessment. I cannot take what is positive about hypermediated writing without accepting the consequences of the negative. Thus, the technotopic will never be as good as promised, nor will the technophobic be as bad.

As such, writing teachers and assessors are developing outcomes and criteria for hypermedia to measure and communicate values associated with bringing multiple communication modes and media together. In *New Media Writing*, Anne Wysocki (2004) encourages those participating in teaching hypermedia to "stay alert to *how* and *why* we make these combinations of materials, not simply *that* we do it" (p. 19). At the level of writing in the classroom, *why* to me seems to matter more than *how*. The *why* question on which Wysocki focuses is the rhetorical rationale for decisions writers make when composing in hypermedia. While hypermedia composition in its multiplicity of forms resonates with many in the discipline, many teachers struggle with how to assess it. Before suggesting specific strategies, I will turn first to examine three common but insufficient approaches to assessing hypermedia.

> *Treating hypermedia the same as print texts.* I was able to make the transition to photo, audio, and video essays relatively early because in my initial exploration of hypermedia, I was struck by the rhetorical nature of these texts and the similar language I could use to discuss the processes by which writers compose in different communicative modes and media. Especially when I looked at something like my writing outcomes, I could imagine many productive areas of overlap where my existing class might connect with student-produced digital texts. However, while these established criteria form a reasonable starting point, they are not sufficient for assessing hypermedia. Cheryl

E. Ball (2006) details her frustration trying to assess hypermedia. The frameworks she drew from all tended to emphasize description, interpretation, and analysis rather than criteria that measured the effectiveness of the relationships between and among modes. My experience confirms her conclusion that we cannot read, understand, and assess hypermedia texts in the same ways and with the same criteria we used for print texts.

Importing criteria from other disciplines. After one determines that the established outcomes and criteria for print texts do not perfectly adapt to assessing hypermedia, a common reaction is to leave the field altogether and search for criteria from other disciplines to add to existing frameworks. Surely graphic communications, film and media studies, visual arts, or other fields have codified criteria from which we can borrow to evaluative the hypertechs that students are composing in writing classes. Madeleine Sorapure (2006), however, warns against drawing writing assessment criteria from other disciplines. While acknowledging that writing teachers often revert to the standards of print literacies, she is equally wary about "borrowing" rules and models from other disciplines, for fear that rhetoric would be in danger of being lost. Plus, she reminds us that assessment is all about context, which needs to consider a wide range of factors, including the course, the students, the teacher, the assignment, the modes, and the medium. While related fields might provide some useful ideas to develop criteria to inform writing assessments, during this time of growth and change, we need to stay grounded in what we know and what we can contribute to the conversation.

Developing reductive grading rubrics. When we venture into unfamiliar pedagogical and assessment territory, we often resort to methods that evoke confidence and security instead of allowing for a measure of ambiguity. Few things in writing assessment appear as objective and certain as a grading rubric. Bob Broad (2003) succinctly reminds us of the trade-off that is all too common when we use rubrics: "In pursuit of their normative and formative purposes, traditional rubrics achieve evaluative *brevity* and *clarity*. In so doing, they surrender their *descriptive* and *informative* potential: responsiveness, detail, and complexity in accounting for how writing is actually evaluated" (p. 2). Hypermedia can be disconcerting for our students, who are often anxious about these assignments. Not to define the criteria for the project prior to assigning it could be unfair or, worse, irresponsible. While many a writing teacher has had an ideal image in his or her mind about what a text should be without clearly communicating it, students should not have to resort to mind reading to receive clear expectations and assessment criteria.

Because hypermedia texts are relatively new, there is an even greater temptation to adopt an attitude of discovering what I like (or don't like) only when I see it. For most hypermedia assignments, I begin by tapping into this list of assessment criteria that build from my course outcomes, acknowledging the rhetoric of negotiating and combining texts:

Holistic Elements:

- Depth of content: conceptual value
- Persuasiveness
- Relationship between modes, media, and texts
- Relationship to traditional conventions
- Organization, arrangement, and progression
- Attention to audience and context

Specific Targeted Elements:

- Progression/pace
- Selection and presentation of found or original images
- Clarity and strength of written content
- Clarity and strength of audio component
- Editing: words, visuals, technology
- Functionality

My responses to students' work are drawn from this list. The list does not dictate my responses, but rather guides and frames them. Here is an example of an e-mail response that I wrote to a particularly good podcast from one of my students.

Feedback/Response Sheet for Podcast
Advanced Article and Essay Workshop
Name: Brittany

Before I get into the formal evaluation, one word: fabulous!

Focus/Angle:
Comments: I saw the overarching theme/concept of the podcast as a type of hybrid review with elements of rich description and

personal narrative. I felt like I was getting the best of a club review, but presented in a way that was far more creative and engaging than most. The balance was ideal, and I can't wait to see/hear/read the longer version in the multimedia essay.

Organization and Arrangement:
Comments: This is one of the high points in a project that was consistently strong. You absolutely hook the listener in the intro-duction with the description of the location and the "journey" to get there. You have a wonderful energy that drew me into the scene. Once you get to the body of the piece, there might have been a bit of a letdown, but instead you kept up the rich description and layered the music in under your narration. My initial move might have been to have music throughout the piece, but your choice was much better. You used it to help the listener enter the scene. If there is one section that might use a bit of tweaking in terms of content, I thought the way you numbered the three elements that made the club unique lost a bit of the tone you established in the piece, though I agree with each of the points. Concluding by tying the ending back to beginning is an effective stylistic move (though I'm trying to remember how Moses "saw the light" from the intro; I think of him along the lines of the 10 Commandments/Red Sea/plagues . . . Have you thought of building around a related theme?).

Progression/Pace/Transitions:
Comments: Good progression throughout. The narrative kept my interest, and you moved seamlessly from one section to the next. For a short piece, I thought you spent about the right amount of time on each part. Because of the potential with the next project, I'm anxious to see if you'll tie in more of your experiences that you wrote about in the first write-up. Now that you have the focus set, you might be able to mine that for especially the interactions at the club. (BTW: This was a significant improvement upon your initial observation in terms of depth of detail and description.)

Clarity and Strength of Word Choice:
Comments: Without having the script in front of me, it's harder to comment on specifics. Overall, I found your word choice com-pelling, direct, and powerful. The action and descriptions were palpable. I don't feel like you wasted any wording, with the slight exception of the numbering I mentioned earlier.

Audience Awareness/Rhetorical Sophistication:
I felt like your efforts to connect with the listener paid off greatly.
You mentioned in class that you have stage experience, and it shows.
Not only did you read expressively, there's something about the
way it sounded almost like a rich, descriptive review that makes it
seem like you have a specific audience and purpose in mind. As far
as I'm concerned, if I hadn't already been to the club, I'd want to go
now . . . In fact, it makes me want to go back sooner than later.

Grade: A
I seriously enjoyed listening to the audio as well as seeing where
this project started and where it is now. It's clear that you have a
renewed focus and purpose for the piece. I know Tuesday is early
to workshop, but see what you can put together for that class. If
you're not opposed, perhaps you'd want to start by playing this
and then move into how the vision will evolve for the multimedia
piece.

Although criteria are slightly different from those listed earlier, it illustrates how I use the criteria to help me organize my response and prepare
students for the way I will evaluate a text that is not typical of their experiences in school. Cynthia Selfe (2004) suggests something similar in *Writing
New Media*, where she suggests including a continuum moving from weak
to strong on which she places an X for an immediate, visual judgment.
The bulk of her feedback is written in the comments space for the descriptive evaluation and response.

Finally, in assessing student hypermedia I have rediscovered the
value of student reflection. The criteria I typically find most vital requires
students to explain their rationale, critical-thinking, decision-making processes, self assessment, or insights into objectives and goals for me to provide meaningful feedback. Although I would not suggest that a specific
communicative mode, medium, or a combination of them is always better
than another, I think that some might be more effective or appropriate
than others, depending on the context and the rhetorical situation. Thus I
understand that part of an author's work is to determine the appropriate
content, modalities, and media to most effectively communicate with his
or her audience; likewise, the work of the evaluator continues to provide
robust, engaged responses and evaluation that acknowledges the rhetorical sophistication of hypermedia composition.

In assessing student hypermedia, several key principles have
emerged from my reading and practice that provide for some concluding axioms:

- Develop criteria for hypermedia that communicate meaningful formative and evaluative feedback.
- Allow for flexibility and multiple ways to successfully combine media and modalities.
- (Re)center hypermedia on rhetorical principles.
- Direct students toward meaningful reflection at multiple stages in the composing process.

HYPERATTENTION

The last of the three characteristics of the digital revolution of writing texts and technologies explored in this chapter is hyperattention. This feature is distinct from hypertext and hypermedia in that it is not textual but rather an attribute of writers and readers in the digital age. While the first two are debated in relation to their place in composition and writing classes, both seem to build on rhetorical principles that have long been part of the discipline and both are highly visible in the manner literacy happens outside school in the 21st century. Hyperattention, though, is more controversial, and it seems to threaten the way we have approached composition and writing in the academy.

N. Katherine Hayles (2007) describes hyperattention as "characterized by switching focus rapidly between different tasks, preferring multiple information streams, seeking a high level of stimulation, and having a low tolerance for boredom" (p. 187). She contrasts hyperattention with deep attention, which has long been valued in academic writing. Although we can see its effects in hypertexts and hypermedia, hyperattention is a physiological characteristic of people who have been influenced by digital texts. In fact, Hayles suggests that the human brain may be physically changing in response to digital texts and technologies. While I have neither the authority nor the expertise to comment on the physiological evidence of this change, I am familiar with the digital texts to which she refers and have many examples of students' composing that represent the characteristics she lists. Controversially, Hayles argues that faculty should not judge students harshly for the shift in composing practice resulting from this evolution; instead, she argues that we need to acknowledge that hyperattention is a reality in literacy and cognition for a new generation of students.

Not surprisingly many academics find hyperattention troubling, having traditionally valued and defined success through writing academic texts representative of deep attention. Writing outcomes uphold the importance of students' ability to stay focused on a main idea in a text, develop points in relation to a larger rhetorical purpose, and arrange ideas within a logical progression. Hyperattention seems to challenge those core values. Further, teachers often resent the pressure to entertain a population of students who cannot seem to focus for longer than a few minutes on a task and who are not audiovisually stimulated by classroom settings with human interaction rather than flashing screens and pulsing audio soundtracks. A false nostalgia recalls "the good ole days" of school when students did not have attention deficit disorder and did not expect their classroom experience to be modeled after digital gaming experiences. There is a long tradition in composition and rhetoric of considering the writer's investment and engagement.

George Hillocks (1995) writes about disaffected and disengaged students and suggests ways to encourage them to invest in their writing (pp. 15–22). Literacy researchers, from Shirley Brice Heath to Beverly Moss to Deborah Brandt, have written accounts of literacy practices of people having much more success with complicated literacy events outside school than they did in school, especially when they have personal reasons to invest in literacy practices. Compositionists have developed pedagogies around student-centered classrooms for years, tapping into student knowledge, expertise, and interests. Although they have much to learn and can develop their skills, students should not be dismissed or blamed because they do not share interests and values with faculty. Student interest may not be the sole criterion to use in developing curriculum and pedagogy, it is not something to dismiss without consideration either.

Many who currently teach did not have formative reading and literacy experiences in digital environments, though that is changing rapidly. Many younger professionals and graduate students are digital natives; even so, I find myself relating to writing in ways that increasingly fit Hayle's definition of hyperattention. I long for the time when I could think, research, read, and write in long chunks of uninterrupted time within a single medium and modality. But when exactly was that time for me? When I was a child? No, growing up I loved reading picture books, vinyl records that would ding when it was time to flip the page of the accompanying book, or books that I could read along with the cassette tape. When I was in elementary, middle, or high school? No, most of my writing that I have saved includes pictures I drew to accompany the writing, charts and graphs, or projects that I presented orally at some event. How about my collegiate career? Even in my earlier college days, I was using a word processor, though it was not WYSIWYG—what you see is what you get—technology (the screen showing an exact representation of what will print). One had to remember an inordinate number of function button commands to do simple tasks like indent a paragraph or underline a word. Early word processing contained visual coding that would disappear, and it was challenging to determine how a document would look before printing. The same transition is happening within Web publishing, where knowing HTML coding is increasingly less important to the average student writer. Computers evolved rapidly during my college career and several of my faculty integrated media into our studies. I watched hours of soccer on Spanish television as part of my language lab, though I enjoyed the games more than I learned the language.

Certainly my dissertation would have been a time of deep attention, wasn't it? No, I wrote most of it in the wee hours between feedings for my newborn twins. I was also teaching and on the job market, so I rarely had the opportunity to focus for long periods. Perhaps as a tenure-line assistant professor writing this book, I finally exhibited deep attention. No, I wrote much of it in spurts over time, with constant interruptions (some self-imposed). When I needed to locate a source or idea, I could open a new electronic window, check a quick citation, or request a book from the library. More than once, students, children, or an intense desire to make a move in my Facebook chess match drew me from the task at hand.

This is the world in which we live, and it's the world in which authors write texts. Perhaps the experiences of a new generation of students and scholars are more acute, with the sheer number of wireless devices and other gadgets, screens, and applications they use, but I would suggest that even the strongest advocates for deep attention would be surprised by how much their literacy practices are marked by hyperattention.

Hyperattention shows a preference and ability to process multiple information streams. Having heard so much about the ability of younger generations to process multiple messages, I decided to do a mini-experiment at a recent conference. While I was talking about Hayle's definition of hyperattention, I started a video of my playing a game with my children. I thus forced the audience to make a choice between three options: continue to listen to the live me give my presentation, shift attention to the sound and sights of the video, or attempt to process both information streams simultaneously. I have to admit that I did a few things to "fix" the experiment. In the video I was playing Nintendo DS Brain Age II with help from my children, who tend to be a natural draw for audiences. Brain Age II is a game with mental calisthenics that are supposed to be performed daily to exercise the mind so that when tested, the user can get closer to what the game considers the ideal brain age: 20. (While I may be wistful for my 20-year-old body, I would strongly resist classifying my 20-year-old brain as at the pinnacle of its performance.) The game we were playing within Brain Age II tests how well a person can hear two to three words spoken simultaneously. The assumption is that the "more youthful" brain can hear and process simultaneous streams of information better than older brains, an assumption that I would not challenge based on my results. Being an academic, I was particularly pleased with myself at the parallel between simultaneous information streams within the video and conference presentation. The assumption is that our minds are changing in response to digital culture, which may enable us to process more information streams simultaneously than those not immersed in digital culture. As one might expect, most of the audience seemed to pay less attention to me in person than they did to the video of the game. While I cannot be certain they were not following both simultaneously, Hayles would suggest that this audience would not be among the demographic of those most likely to be adept at processing multiple stream of information.

Jay David Bolter (2008) has addressed the concept of "multiplicity of forms in hybrid expression," noting that writing is expanding to include multimedia and other forms of composition and composing spaces. He sees a failure of disembodied visions of virtual reality and a shift to hybrid spaces that do not completely "shut out the real world." Instead of envisioning virtual reality as a separate sphere from physical reality, the most interesting work being done combines the virtual and physical worlds. Hybrid virtual reality might look like a person walking down the sidewalk with a special pair of glasses in which one lens is clear and the other is a computer screen. The person negotiating the hybrid space would need to be able to simultaneously track and respond to both spheres at once.

Spaces, though, are just a part of the larger picture of textual hybridization. Students are producing a variety of hybrid digital texts. One particular student-produced text is interesting to consider in relation to its hybridity and its demonstrating how students can compose in multiple communication modes.

Jaclyn transformed what started out as a memoir of her yearly visits to Dodgertown during spring training into a video essay about what Floridians (and regular visitors to Florida during spring training) will miss when the Dodgers move their spring training facilities to Arizona. In addition to her revised personal narrative, Jaclyn included information on how spring baseball is changing, as illustrated by pictures of her and her family at Dodgertown juxtaposed with images of the newer Cracker Jack Stadium, which she calls the "Disney-fied" version of spring training.

To support her message, Jaclyn chose Bruce Springsteen's "Glory Days" to play in the background of the digital video. I know from showing a clip of this video at conferences and workshops that her using a Springsteen song will cause some in the audience to cry foul and dismiss this example, but I do introduce students to fair use and allow them to make informed decisions about the use of copyrighted texts. Informed people disagree on issues of copyright, but I err on the side of students who use texts with full attribution for academic purposes, which is what Jaclyn did as she edited and arranged these texts together in a digital video.

A hybrid text such as this presents interesting rhetorical decisions surrounding the combination of modes and texts that are available to writers/composers in digital environments. For now, suffice it to say that the critical processes of making informed, rhetorically strategic choices are foundational for my class outcomes. As Stroupe (2000) warns, "The mere juxtaposition of words and images, however, would not automatically result in the mutual 'illumination' of languages or forms. Hybridity . . . must not simply be formal or generic, but ideological and historical" (p. 620). If hybrid hypertechs are not all equal in rhetorical effectiveness, sophistication, correctness, and critical thinking, they can and should be assessed in a way that communicates those standards and values to the student composers.

The implications of hyperattention for assessment are potentially the most revolutionary of all hypertechs, yet it is the area about which I am most reticent to push us toward rapid adoption. As related to hypertexts and hypermedia, I see the evolution of writing in the digital age as consistent with the direction we have been moving in as a field. Hypertechs require adjustments to our teaching and to assessment, but the goals and outcomes of the writing class remain relatively consistent. They might challenge the purpose that we might see for composition. For example, if we see composition as preparing student writers for other writing situations on campus in the majors, it is unlikely that hypertexts and hypermedia will reflect the needs most faculty across campus would say students have. However, if the goals of writing classes focus more on rhetorical sophistication and self-consciousness of the writer, the work of hypertechs could be a viable way to achieve such ends. I cannot now claim the same for hyperattention. While I acknowledge that most if not all writers display characteristics of hyperattention in their writing and composing, for the most part we encourage students to produce texts that display deep thinking. I would be uncomfortable, even unwilling, to consider changing the criteria I presently use to assess student writing.

I think this does, though, have at least two practical implications for the writing class. First, if we buy into the idea that hyperattention has become a characteristic of contemporary readers, we need to help student authors consider how this will affect authentic rhetorical situations they will face as writers. Teachers who value deep attention and read for it could cause students to get a false sense of readership. This is already apparent in the ways we advise freshly minted PhDs to significantly revise anything they wrote in their dissertation for publication. Authentic audiences would not tolerate the deep attentive moves we require graduate students to make in their dissertations. The same might be true of writing at other levels. It may be common in an English class for a student to complete 10-, 15-, or even 20-plus papers that appeal to our sense of depth and development that may not be present for readers in other contexts. Students writing for authentic audiences might need to consider low thresholds of boredom and the need for audio and visual stimulation to stay invested.

Second, we need to articulate the value of sustaining a thought, idea, or argument over longer periods than most of our students will be accustomed to when coming into our classes. While their processes might be reflective of hyperattention, their ability to produce texts that carry forward ideas in a focused way will continue to be important to the construction of knowledge. There is no need to think that just because students are making connections between and among elements of their work (hypertext) and negotiating multimedia and communication modalities (hypermedia) that their texts will be necessarily superficial. If we value the depth that might be described as resulting from deep thinking, we need to articulate what that consists of and allow students to demonstrate the multiple ways they might be able to accomplish it via hypertechs.

BECOMING HYPERSENSITIVE

At least three hyper characteristics of writing in the 21st century present significant opportunities and challenges to the current generation of students and teachers, not the least of which is the way we need to assess hypertexts, hypermedia, and hyperattention. While none is completely new to teachers, characteristics of hypertechs are more pronounced in the age of digital texts and technologies and represent the increasing relationship between writing classes and the types of writing that happen outside school. In understanding how hypertechs are, should, or should not influence assessment criteria in writing classes, we need to look at how they promote values we have long held as important for writers, pushing us to rethink what we currently articulate about effective writing, and influencing ways in which writers relate to their subjects, their audiences, and themselves. Hypertext and hypermedia can straightforwardly fit into the current design of most writing classes and programs, especially those focused on such relevant issues as genre, circulation, metacognition, rhetoric, and media. Although each provides its own unique set of issues, and some adjustments are necessary, many writing programs, classes, and teachers are ready to integrate the technologies into their pedagogies and curriculum.

Writing assessments for such high-tech writing should represent not just a fragmented list of new criteria; it should evaluate ways in which connections and multiple media interrelate within the texts. Our assessments should also consider a wide range of rhetorical skills and knowledge required of composers of hypertechs. Hyperattention is the wild card in the equation of hypertechs, though even there multiple information streams and quick shifts of attention are less problematic than the low threshold for boredom and need to stimulation; critical thinking, the ability to focus and develop an argument, and organization and arrangement of ideas as some of the more important outcomes for writing classes.

Inasmuch as hyperattention challenges those core values, it might be worth challenging. However, the inclusion of some of these characteristics will not necessarily lead to unsatisfactory texts. The goal of disciplinary faculty who invest in high-tech teaching environments will be to articulate the criteria for writing assessment that will guide students in worthwhile directions without limiting or dictating the possibilities of what this writing can be for writers and readers. Therefore, the criteria in this chapter and the frameworks in the next are points to consider in the continuing dialogue about how to define effective writing within the realm of hypertechs.

CHAPTER 6

Assessing the Texts and Techs
of the Digital Revolution

The first rule of any technology used in a business is that automation applied to an efficient operation will magnify the efficiency. The second is that automation applied to an inefficient operation will magnify the inefficiency.

—Bill Gates

REGARDLESS OF OUR predisposition toward digital technologies, one thing is certain: They will continue to emerge, reshape, and revolutionize the ways we think about writing and its assessment in the 21st century and beyond. Since digital technologies are becoming more ubiquitous within educational contexts, we as educators, especially those of us who are invested in writing and its delivery to students, must find ways to determine which technologies are worth pursuing and which we should resist. It is less a question of whether or not to embrace digital technologies, and more about the ways they shape the views and practices of writing, teaching, and assessing students as well as which technologies will help us best achieve our articulated curriculum and pedagogy. We know that technological access remains a major issue for educators and students and is partly responsible for the continued hegemony within our educational systems and society at large (Selfe, 1999). Beyond access, significant divisions divide people by how they use available technologies in more or less advantageous ways. Thus, simply infusing educational environments with digital technologies without helping teachers and students understand how to use them in useful ways frames the problem as one that is primarily instrumental and can be solved by granting more equitable access to technologies. Just because technologies reinforce social and education inequities, however, we cannot ignore them or deny their influence. Social injustice will not disappear by our accepting or rejecting the promises of new technologies. Rather, we must use this opportunity to teach students rhetorical and critical approaches to technologies, since they are so much a part of public, private, and commercial life in the United States and since they shape so much of our interaction with texts in and outside school settings.

With whatever technologies are available to us for our writing classes and for the assessment of writing, we still must determine which to embrace and which to reject in response to our curriculum and pedagogy. Keeping up with the rapid emergence of new technologies is a perennial problem for educators. Even when we have financial resources, it is difficult to find time or, for those educators with expertise, to evaluate the options and determine where to best invest our energies. New technologies emerge so quickly that by the time we integrate one into our writing classes or assessments, others are already begging to be considered, prompting educators to either uncritical acceptance or rejection of new technologies. But those who do persevere often do so in order to engage students, who are constantly exploring new technologies. Educators cannot afford the reputation of being behind the curve. Even the desire to meet students where they are can be a challenge, since integrating digital applications into classes is among the surest ways to guarantee that students will migrate to something new. Much like the trends we have seen in music over the past several decades, part of the appeal of new technologies for students is that spaces have not been co-opted by authorities. Therefore, whatever technologies we adopt for teaching and learning are sure to be outdated almost as soon as we bring them into the classroom.

For instance, I have heard undergraduate students talking between classes about how Facebook has been ruined because their mothers, aunts, family members, and teachers are all signing on. Facebook's internal statistics confirm these students' worst fears. As of February 2009, women over 55 constitute the area of greatest growth, up 175% in the previous 120 days ("Fastest," 2009). With no offense to this particular demographic, this growth does not bode well for the "hipness" factor of the technology. Where students will land next is for them to know and us to find out, and when we do, they will be ready to move on to something else. While it is still generally positive for educators to include authentic writing situations for students into our classes, educators will necessarily be a step or two behind them regardless of how quickly we try to incorporate new technologies.

Having the mentality that we need to keep up with every new writing and assessment technology ultimately sets us up for exhaustion at best, failure at worst, and either way the depletion of valuable time and financial resources. Despite a renewed snobbery among technology enthusiasts even in our discipline, I think it is important to give ourselves permission not to jump on every technological bandwagon that comes along. At the risk of personal embarrassment, loss of ethos, and incurring the wrath of smart colleagues, I will admit that I have yet to embrace the Twitter phenomenon, though I understand that some people use it in their writing classes in ways that I find compelling. It has been a conscience choice for me as a teacher, and at the moment I do not feel inclined to move in that direction beyond the analysis of the ways the technology influences circulation, in cases such as President Obama's use of Twitter during the 2008 election campaign, for example, or in reportage of world events. In choosing whether to use a technology in a writing class, the thinking and the rationale is more crucial than the conclusion.

For instance, can I provide a coherent rationale for why I use blogs, wikis, Listservs, e-mail, discussion boards, file sharing, electronic comments, digital video, digital audio, and digital editing programs in my class—but not Twitter? Is it a good enough reason that I am slightly annoyed by the self-obsessive navel gazing of a generation of writers? Am I put off because I think that much of the reporting in these spaces is posturing? Do I think that the concept of "followers" smacks of megalomania? Is it the limit on characters per tweet that makes it something I do not want to promote in my writing class à la my critique of hyperattention in the previous chapter? Whatever the answers, I should have a reason related to my course, curriculum, pedagogy, or program that allows me to answer these and other related questions unless I am willing to admit the arbitrary nature of my decisions.

The decisions many of us make about writing and assessment technologies are not arbitrary, but we may find it challenging to articulate a rationale without a framework or way to help systematically process what is at stake. We know we cannot include every technology into our classes and that we do not want to fall into the assumption of the technological imperative—if a technology is available, we ought to use it. Decisions are further complicated because if we choose to pursue new technologies, we know it will be at the expense of something else in our current model. By including hypertechs in our classes and assessment systems, we fear that we will need to abandon more traditional texts and tests and that we might lose something in the transaction. In conversations with writing teachers on all levels, I hear the concern that we are going to lose something fundamental about reading and writing if we abandon print literacies. It is important, then, to consider not just what is gained by including certain digital technologies into our writing courses but also what we may lose. The benefits may outweigh the costs in some cases but not in others, which is why we have to carefully consider the consequences of digital texts and technologies.

I suggest two frameworks that can help us answer questions surrounding which technologies to include in our writing classes and writing assessment systems. The first is a unified validity framework that draws directly on the best work in educational and writing assessment that defines a test's validity through the accuracy, appropriateness, and social consequences of decisions made based on assessment results (Broad, 2003; Cronbach, 1989; Huot, 2002; Messick, 1989; Moss, 1992; Penrod, 2005). Validity measurements are the ways we assess assessments. The second framework draws connections between course outcomes (what students should be able to do at the end of a defined period of time) and the affordances of specific technologies. Using this filter, the technologies would have to demonstrably help the student achieve ends that we have determined will be central to our courses in the 21st century. After explaining the frameworks, I conclude by establishing several principles to guide writing experts in decisions about which digital technologies are worth pursuing within the context of local needs, student and teacher populations, and educational goals.

CONSTRUCT VALIDITY AS A MEANS OF ASSESSING HYPERTECHS

As mentioned briefly in Chapter 1, validity is the crucial concept in writing assessment, but it is often used in ways that distract from its core values. I have seen three prevalent responses within rhetoric and composition discourage a robust and applicable understanding of the term: (1) defining validity simply as "if a test measures what it purports to measure," (2) favoring reliability over validity, and (3) dismissing validity as either too abstract or difficult. The most common definitions of validity center on truthfulness: "Validity has to do with honesty and accuracy, with a demonstrated connection between what a test proclaims it is measuring and what it in fact measures" (White, 1993, p. 90). I like *honesty* as a word choice here, since in its evocation, it signals that some tests are honest while others are not (or at least less than completely honest if we want to measure at that level). But what does that mean? It is important, for instance, that tests that once claimed to measure intelligence, aptitude, or innate ability change their claims, since they were misleading educators and the public. Transparency has not been the hallmark of assessment within educational contexts.

But even this definition of validity begs the questions, How does one determine if an assessment, or an assessment technology, is honest or dishonest? How do we know if it does what it claims to do? Historically these questions have been answered by categorizing a number of ways one could determine validity, each representing an attribute of its honesty. However, the subcategories existed outside a larger context with none being sufficient in and of itself. Thus validity was often mis-used by allowing a subcategory of validity to be substituted for a more comprehensive claim. Although the American Psychological Association (APA) guidelines established that the branches of validity should function together—"Aspects of validity can be discussed independently, but only for convenience. They are interrelated operationally and logically; only rarely is one of them alone important in a particular situation" (American Educational Research Association, American Psychological Association, and National Council on Measurement in Eucation, 1985, p. 26)—validity was often understood and claimed by separating it into its smaller parts. As a result assessments are often generically deemed valid based on their compliance to a specific branch of validity without being measured within a more comprehensive context. In this way, assessments "get away with" confidently claiming validity, given that few stakeholders have the neces-sary background in educational assessment to understand the nuances of their definition or to challenge the assertion. Because of their history and influence as the dominant discourse, test companies have the apparatus and political clout necessary to silence voices of dissent or those with new ideas for assessing student writing.

Although none of the many subcategories of validity was sufficient to stand alone, three branches of validity emerged that were deemed most significant. Lorie Shepard (1993) provides an overview of the branches from APA's classification system that became what she calls the "trinitar-ian doctrine" of validity: content validity, criterion-related validity, and construct validity. *Content validity* includes the scope of material covered in an assessment, which in determining it, the assessor turns his or her attention to ways the questions represent a larger body of skills or knowl-edge. *Criterion-related validity* is to what extent the test scores correlate with external factors such as other tests, grades, or future performances outside the test. The third branch of validity, *construct validity*—not to be confused with *unified construct validity*—has four features: (1) the relation-ship between the test and other variables, (2) experimental evidence as well as the more commonly collected correlational data, (3) consideration of reasonable competing hypotheses, and (4) its application (pp. 415–417). Even with these three main branches of validity that were supposed to work together in the evaluation, validity arguments still favored fragmen-tation and thus communicated results in ways that were less than honest and left the need for a more comprehensive concept.

The second way that even experts within the discipline mistreat validity is in its relation to reliability. Reliability is most often understood as a necessary but insufficient condition for validity (Cherry & Meyer, 1993) and is often used to justify the elevation of reliability over validity.

Reliability is often preferable to validity, since measures of consistency are quantifiable, which appeals to those with a scientistic disposition. If anything can silence opposing views on innovative writing assessments better than existing social, historical, and political forces, it is statistical measurement, because it is widely accepted within educational and societal contexts as impervious to subjectivity. Once the consistency of an assessment is statistically determined (regardless of what consistency it is measuring), any one of the branches of validity is cited to solidify the claim rather than provide any meaningful input into the evaluation. The burden of proof reliability provides often outranks and overshadows a more balanced view of validity as required by the APA. This bias has trickled down even into rhetoric and composition, even though many of us do not accept its underlying assumptions. However, the relationship between reliability and validity has been used and repeated so often that it has become a truism in the field.

Finally, rhetoric and composition experts, long perplexed by the debates within writing assessment circles about validity, can too often see discussions around validity as an abstract or meaningless debate within a subdiscipline rather than linked to something useful for classes and programmatic purposes. Much of the disinterest in the field at large is our fault as assessment experts. We have become so attuned to the implications of validity and reliability that we take for granted that not everyone shares this interest. Also, because much of the debate on validity occurs within an educational assessment community that has a steep learning curve of technical language, ability to read and interpret statistics, and sociological epistemologies, we too often do not consider how our work in assessment might appear isolated from other work in the discipline. I remember vividly a Conference on College Composition and Communication (CCCC) session on validity in the early 2000s in which some of the best assessment scholars in the field unpacked the core values of validity in ways that had enormous implications for writing assessment. I was listening and taking notes in the hallway—the room was filled beyond capacity. After members of the panel presented their arguments, one of the most well-known and trusted figures in our discipline was called on to respond to what he had heard. To my chagrin, but not that of many around me, it seemed, his response was that all this talk about validity was too difficult and that we should return to our simpler definition: that validity is a measure of whether a test measures what it claims to measure. Despite our efforts we often do not accomplish our goals when we are talking about validity and assessment.

While validity requires careful consideration and has more nuance than what I will present here, I would respectfully disagree. In fact, I think it can provide a framework that can help us at a most fundamental level in determining which digital assessment technologies to include in our writing classes, curriculum, and pedagogy. Samuel Messick (1989) provides a definition of unified construct validity that bring together the separate branches in a way that is both comprehensive and accessible: "Validity is an overall evaluative judgment of the degree to which empirical evidence and theoretical rationales support the *adequacy* and *appropriateness* of *interpretations* and *actions* based on test scores or other modes of assessment" (p. 5). Within this accessible definition, three principles emerge that can become a framework to assess available writing and assessment technologies.

1. *Validity is an evaluation of a decision, not of a test or technology.* Writing assessment data cannot speak for itself; rather it is interpreted by people (Cronbach, 1971). As we saw in Chapter 1, within a traditional framework of assessment, assessors look to the instruments or the data produced by the instrument as if they dictated educational decisions rather than people. If admissions into an honors program were determined solely by the number on a standardized test score, it would appear as if educators had no role in selecting students for admittance into the program. If scholarships were granted only to students who achieved a particular test score, it might appear as if the score selected students for the opportunity. In both cases, while the instrument or the data from the assessment may seem to allow or prevent students access to educational opportunities, people are responsible for determining how to use these or other scores. In many cases, scores are used to relieve educators from considering the individual needs and skills of students. In other cases, they are used to prevent educators from being able to make meaningful decisions about students. In either case assessments or their scores appear to wield more authority than people and do not invite or allow human expertise or consideration. Assessment technologies that produce numbers or scores as a final determination instead of educators making decisions about students, their needs, and their writing works against the principles of humane writing assessment and should be avoided. At the core of effective writing assessment is meaningful communication between students and educators, and validity is the measure of human decisions, not a test instrument or a number.

   This objective facade of test scores and instruments is not used only for large-scale assessment decisions within institutions and classes. Many teachers use quantifiable assessment procedures, such as numerical grading rubrics, to score student writing. Once numbers are assigned in the respective categories and they are tallied up, the rubric and scale dictate the evaluation (e.g., a student receives 44 of a possible 50 points using the grading rubric, so the grade assigned is automatically an 88% or a B+). The individual making the assessment decision, in this case the classroom teacher, can either be overridden by or hidden behind the objectivity and quantification of the rubric. No matter how many barriers educators construct to shield themselves from taking responsibility for assessment decisions, they determine the appropriateness, accuracy, and use of the assessment and thus assume responsibility for the validity of a test when they make decisions based upon the results of the assessment. Of course we must be careful in assigning blame. Many educators desire and are prepared to make decisions about students but are prevented from doing so because of a system that mistrusts them and purposefully robs them of their capacity to make humane decisions about students based on their needs.

A better approach to assessment acknowledges and embraces human decision making and the inevitable subjectivity of writing assessments. Within this framework, assessors are allowed to make decisions about students and their writing and required to be appropriately informed about students and their writing. Human readers cannot hope to respond to a student text mechanically, objectively, and completely consistently. As Pamela Moss (1994) notes, subjectivity within this framework acknowledges the assumptions and beliefs that might effect the interpretation of a text: "The reader's preconceptions, 'enabling' prejudices, or foreknowledge are inevitable and valuable in interpreting a text. In fact they make understanding possible" (p. 7). Because subjectivity will necessarily exist in any human interpretation of a text, it is better to acknowledge it and include it in the overall assessment rather than to attempt to ignore or eliminate it. One important consideration in determining the assessment technologies we use in writing classes is the extent to which they allow for, require, and make visible the human decision-making processes and the way it enables communication between educators and students rather than hiding the scoring processes and appropriating agency from students and educators.

2. *Validity is an argument measured by degree, not statistical determination dominated by reliability.* Within a traditional writing assessment framework, validity is reported as either achieving or being denied the status of validity. Because the either/or decision must be defended, the proposition is often measured largely by quantifiable variables to objectify the taxonomy. Within unified construct validity, the appropriateness

and accuracy of decisions are understood as a matter of degree, not as oppositional binary. Again, this is something we have known for some time, but it has yet to be adopted widely within educational settings: "The term *validity* is derived from the Latin *valere*, meaning 'to be strong.' The derivation from the concept of strength suggests that validity is an axiological matter of degree, not a positivistic dichotomy of valid versus invalid. . . . Strictly speaking, it is nonsense to assert that a given assessment is valid or invalid" (Scharton, 1996, p. 55). Refreshingly, this plays into our strengths as rhetoricians. Familiar to those of us in composition and rhetoric, this type of validation can be compared to an argument measured by strength or degree. An argument is more or less persuasive, depending on the reasoning and evidence used to support it. The claims can be strengthened or weakened by a variety of factors without necessitating a binary determination of right or wrong. In the same way that we know that topics on which students write are often not either/or propositions, so validity arguments should be nuanced, and we should be able to speak back to them in meaningful ways. Likewise a validity argument can be strengthened or weakened by the evidence used to support the decision.

In terms of a framework for determining which assessment technologies to adopt within our institutions, programs, and classes, we should be wary of any claims that an assessment is simply valid or invalid, especially if that determination has been made based on statistical evidence. There is no magic number that makes a test or technology valid or invalid. Discussions of validity should be arguments, in the most productive sense of the word, and should be based on evidence that is negotiated between stakeholders. Much of the rhetoric behind traditional assessment relies on silencing students, teachers, and anyone who questions the appropriateness or accuracy of the measure. That is not true of unified construct validity, nor should it be about the assessment technologies we develop and adopt in our programs and classes.

An important factor in this discussion is that we must know the appropriate way to consider reliability within assessment technologies. Reliability can serve an important purpose, but we must reframe what that is and acknowledge that consistency plays out in a variety of ways in any assessment technology and that not all are equal or even necessary. Herald Berlak (1992b) uses an instrumental metaphor to explain reliability: "Using the thermometer analogy, reliability is established if the instrument can be shown to give nearly identical temperature readings, plus or minus a small and predictable margin of error, when used repeatedly under the same conditions" (p. 183). His metaphor draws on a scientific paradigm in which the variables in the assessment system can be isolated and controlled and where there is a phenomenon that is knowable and measurable. If all other variables are completely consistent, the instrument or multiple instruments should produce consistent readings without error. In this view, reliability resides within the instrument and its ability to accurately report a knowable reality.

Our understanding of students and their writing, however, does not draw necessarily on a positivist, scientific epistemology in the same way as the measurement of temperature. If my wife and I read the same book but have a different response to it, I would not consider either of our readings to be an error. Or if I reread the book a year later, I will necessarily bring a new perspective to the text, which is why I read important texts multiple times. Since I discover something new each time, my reading and response to it will not be consistent. Only in reading for writing assessments do we tend to construct these phenomena as errors or problems to be corrected. It is this limited understanding of reading and response that leads to the conclusion that machines are superior to human readers, since the former always approach texts in the same way according to their programming.

Reliability in writing assessment most often means interrater reliability, or consistency between scorers. Once a statistically significant level of interrater reliability is reached, assessment experts often conclude that the score is accurate and appropriate. While this is only one type of consistency within an assessment system, it is attractive to testing companies, since it can be easily determined, quantified, and employed to support—or in some cases be a substitute for—the validity of an assessment. It is also something that they know highly mechanized systems address well.

In other words, reliability plays into the strengths of mechanistic assessment technologies. If student texts are run through computers programmed to count and assign scores in exactly the same way, it is not difficult to imagine that they will be perfectly consistent. This is what a machine would do best. If reliability becomes a substitute for or the primary measure of validity, it clearly favors the mechanized system over the human reader. Statistically significant measures of reliability may not even be necessary in every assessment decision to establish validity (Huot, 1990; Moss, 1994). While this might seem blasphemous to some—I receive astonished looks from many administrators and educational assessment specialists trained in psychometric, as if I have just claimed that indeed the world is flat rather than round— we need to find ways to prevent reliability from gaining undue influence over the assessment technologies we use within our programs and classes. While certain measures of consistency can be important to the decision, often the numbers are used to silence those who would question the appropriateness or accuracy of decisions made about students, teachers, or programs based on assessment results. While the more common mistake with reliability is to give it too much authority in the determination of validity, the other is to ignore reliability because it has been previously misused to dominate the decision making. While *reliability* is not an irrelevant term, it has to be framed within the overall context of the assessment. It is one piece of evidence within the larger context of the decision that must be weighed and considered in relationship to other factors.

One of the big questions I ask about any new assessment technology is how it treats inconsistency and what happens when different determinations are made within the system. It is at these points of dissonance that some of the most valuable work within writing assessments can take place. If my reading of a student's paper is different from those of other students in the class, this dissonance can become an important moment of teaching and learning for the students and me. Many of us have had the experience of receiving a complaint from a student based on our different evaluation of a text in relationship to other students in a workshop, another teacher, or even a student's parents. Presumably, these other parties bolstered the students' confidence by indicating that the paper was wonderful, whereas our reading was decidedly less positive. In this case the student appeals to his or her sense of unfairness based on inconsistency. In the student's logic, if he or she received certain responses from others, my reading and evaluation should align with that of the group. The student is perfectly right to be confused and appeal to a sense of fairness. Here is what we can both learn in a situation like this. I can learn about the ways other audiences respond to the student's writing, which may or may not provide an alternative lens through which to view his or her work. The student can learn, as well, that I might have a different reading from those of others and that I have a vested interest in certain principles that we may be covering in the class. It does not mean that my reading is always correct, but rather that it may be informed by different assumptions and a different set of criteria as the classroom teacher. Once the student and I both realize that no two readings will be identical, we are both in a better place to examine why people will respond to his or her writing in varying ways.

Consistency in large-scale assessments can be equally nuanced, though it may be more difficult to support institutionally. In my experience of administrating assessments, I have had the opportunity to work with faculty with different backgrounds, experiences, and expectations for student writing. Drawing on models established by William Smith and Bob Broad, faculty expertise and communication become the basis for the assessment rather than mechanistic calibration of scorers. In one case, for example, when I was administrating an assessment for a writing-across-the-curriculum event, several newer teachers from English learned that effective writing in engineering and the sciences often uses passive voice as a way to emphasize the object rather than the actor. Experts in that discipline confirmed that they considered this acceptable, even preferable, in many cases, since it foregrounded the object rather than the subject in the sentence. If a engineering student writes, "Two milliliters of sulfuric acid were added to the mixture of . . . ," it communicates the more essential element of the sentence better than the active construction. This revelation is not earth shattering for those of us who have taught technical or professional communication, but these new English teachers would have missed the opportunity to learn something if their reading had been classified as an error and disregarded. Talking about inconsistencies in the way we evaluate and judge writing often leads to a productive and helpful exchange. Writing assessments are a location for teaching and learning for faculty and students alike when they are approached in ways that acknowledge the humanness of reading and the assumptions we bring to the table as readers. How would a machine score the passive voice of the engineering text? I suppose that would depend on how it was programmed, but I will note that grammar checkers regularly flag such constructions as errors. Perhaps more important, machines are unable to engage in discussion and thinking about rhetorical reasons that writers might use the passive voice in different contexts. They count passive voice as either correct or incorrect depending on how they are programmed. They score at impressively high levels of consistency, as if that were the main problem, but they have no sense of reasoning through the rhetorical situation.

3. *Appropriateness must be factored into the validity argument, including an analysis of the social and educational consequences of using the technology.* In addition to the accuracy of the decision, which tends to be the primary focus of validity claims, we must also consider the appropriateness of the assessment to make specific decisions about students, teachers, and institutions. Students' lives are affected by the results of assessment decisions: They receive grades and degrees; they gain (or fail to gain) admission to universities or programs; they gain (or are denied) access to financial resources such as grants, loans, or scholarships; and they

are sorted into educational paths that might direct their future prospects. Teachers are evaluated according to how their students perform on assessments; some might receive more (or fewer) opportunities for advancement, pay, or other benefits resulting from assessment data; and curricula are shaped in response to high-stakes assessment systems. While the previous points have addressed accuracy, we have not looked systematically at the appropriateness of assessment decisions, especially in relation to the intended or unintended consequences that accompany them.

Appropriateness can take many forms in an assessment system, one of which centers on the authenticity of the writing task. For years educators questioned why multiple-choice tests taken over a few hours on a Saturday morning should be a chief component of determining collegiate access at institutions across the country. Writing experts questioned how vocabulary and reading-comprehension tests should substitute for verbal competence in students. Composition directors similarly question why a test in literature should result in 1st-year composition credit. Somewhere along the way with writing assessment technologies, we have lost sight of the appropriateness of the decision made in relation to the data gathered from the test. Even when direct writing assessments were implemented, many of them suffered from the same lack of self-awareness. Why should we determine a student's placement into or out of writing classes based on a timed writing prompt? Why should students produce texts without their normal tools for composing or support structures? Why should we let unknown raters evaluate student texts for generic scores rather than assess student writing ourselves for local decision making? Why should we sequester graduate students in rooms without access to resources to answer questions for days and even weeks? Why do we attach such weighty decisions to writing produced in inauthentic contexts? We do so because we have let other constraints such as cost, fear of cheating, and time constraints dictate the assessment technology. Until we get a handle on the appropriateness of decisions we make based on assessment results, no digital technology will be sufficient.

The social and educational consequences that result from decisions made within an assessment system are an important part of measuring appropriateness. As we have now witnessed with the Supreme Court ruling on the New Haven firefighters' lawsuit, employers can no longer legally consider the negative social consequences of employment or promotion tests to determine their accuracy or appropriateness. Perhaps the justices in this case need a refresher course on the Jim Crow laws of reconstruction. In her dissent, Ruth Bader Ginsburg asserted, "Congress endeavored to promote equal opportunity in fact, and not simply in form. The damage today's decision does to that objective is untold." While specific social consequences can be purposefully built into assessment systems—as we now know about early IQ and standardized aptitude tests that specifically normed tests so that men outscored women (Mensh & Mensh, 1991; Mercer, 1989)— more often than not their negative consequences are unintentional side effects of assessment systems that are developed with more benevolent origins. However, that does not relieve us of our responsibility to determine the consequences and act appropriately to our findings. While many assessment scholars have called for consideration of social consequences related to assessment systems (Camp, 1993; Messick, 1989; Moss, 1992; Shepard, 1993), in complex social and educational systems, simple cause-and-effect relationships do not exist. Therefore, we must take the time to consider the long-term as well as the short-term consequences of the writing assessments we adopt to make educational decisions. This measure must become an ongoing process of inquiry built into our institutions, programs, and classes.

So how does an educator include a consideration of social consequences into a validity argument? A first step is acknowledging that writing assessments can distribute resources and educational opportunities inequitably. Recently, I administered a summer writing assessment for students that scored a certain number or below on the verbal portion of the SAT. On the one hand, I am pleased that we have something in place locally to look at student writing in order to determine the classes and support structures these students will need to succeed at the institution. This assessment acknowledges that standardized tests scores are not effective indicator for what we need to know. However, the assessment has several drawbacks. While we look at student writing, we do so in an inauthentic environment where students are asked to compose an essay based on a prompt in a 90-minute period without digital writing technologies or resources. This needs to change.

More important, as I walked into the auditorium for the assessment, I was struck by an undeniable visual picture of the racial profiling that result from standardized testing. The room of students was overwhelmingly populated by international and African America students. I felt racist just standing up in front of the group and administrating the assessment, even though this particular writing test could only improve their placement. It may be worth noting anecdotally that this year, 87% of students improved their placements in relation to their standardized-test scores, which would indicate as well how ineffective the initial score is for our local purposes. While I look forward to ways we can improve this assessment in the future, each year it will serve as a visual reminder for me of the gross inequities that can be perpetuated by assessments.

Most educators, however, do not get the experience of walking into an auditorium full of students that provide such a clear visual reminder of the inequities and negative social consequences of assessment technologies. Therefore, the next step—which is decidedly more complex and resource consuming—is to systematically collect data that will help us determine the extent of biases and negative consequences within the writing assessment technologies we use to make decisions. I cannot yet speak knowledgeably of biases associated with my classes and with programs that I have directed, even though their heavy technological integration might be cause to suspect that certain populations of students do better than others. Few of us perhaps have taken the time to consider our own biases, regardless of what factors might lead some students to achieve more than others. Those of us who have increased responsibility for programs and students bear more responsibility to account for their consequences and the ways in which the assessment technologies account for the results. Neither benevolent intentions nor ignorance of adverse social and educational consequences resulting from writing assessment decisions are a viable position for educators in the 21st century.

WRITING OUTCOMES AS A MEANS OF ASSESSING HYPERTECHS

In addition to construct validity as a means to evaluate the appropriateness, accuracy, and social consequences of digital writing and assessment technologies, exploring the relationship between the new technologies and writing outcomes is a framework to help us adopt new technologies. While some in the field are moving away from them, outcomes provide a starting point to talk about the ways in which the content of composition are changing in relation to digital technologies. As Cheryl Ball says in the video *Take 20* (Taylor, 2008), the four categories initially presented in the Writing Program Administrators (WPA) outcomes provide a springboard for her to think about ways she integrates technologies into her composition classes:

> One of the things I did recently was look at the WPA outcomes statement for first year writing, and I tweaked it for what happens if those list of four outcomes for writing classes were applied not just to written texts but to new media or multimodal texts. And they kind of shift pretty easily into that, and

they could currently accommodate different kinds of communication besides written alphabetic texts. (Taylor, 2008)

Digital texts and technologies are pushing at the outcomes developed several years ago in healthy ways, but they still provide a context to talk and think about the curricular implications of new technologies through this framework. Moreover, many of our writing programs and classes have used and modified these outcomes over the years in ways that reflect the core values of what we study and teach.

Question 1: Which existing outcomes (nationally or in your own program) are connected to a hypertech that you are considering implementing?

For many years writing experts have seen outcomes as a way to define and ascribe values to the work of writing courses. Often these outcomes serve a dual purpose as defining criteria for writing assessment in a particular context. The most prominent effort in defining outcomes is the WPA Outcomes Statement developed by writing faculty interested in supporting colleagues around the country in their efforts to define the scope and purposes of the 1st-year writing experience. In addition to what students should be able to do, it also provides ideas for what faculty should do to support such learning. The WPA Outcomes—and the local outcomes that are often defined in relation to them—are a useful way to think through the inclusion or exclusion of hypertechs, since they identify several larger goals that we have worked toward as a field for many years.

If, for instance, I have just returned from a conference where I have been introduced to a new assessment technology or have just read an article that expounds upon the virtues of a particular assessment technology, and I am interested in implementing it for my class or program, I can begin by looking at my course or program outcomes and connect them back to the technology I am considering. If my program outcomes are such that they can only or best be measured through the new technology, I will probably want to pursue it. If my outcomes do not match up, it might be more suitable to use a different technology. For example, if my current course outcomes require students to interact with one another through digital media, then a networking site might very well be an appropriate hypertech to include in the class. Or if by using the networking system, it gives students the opportunity to meet an outcome such as collaboration or peer critique, perhaps that technology will be a means by which that outcome is achieved. As in every case, though, outcomes can be achieved in a number of ways. In this case students can collaborate and peer critique in many ways that do not include electronically mediated network spaces. Therefore, the question shifts to what the new technology will do to facilitate or otherwise make that interaction better than other options.

Of this one thing I am certain: It is not possible to continue adding hypertechs to the curriculum without making tough choices to substitute them for something else in the class that is either redundant or less important in achieving the ends of the course. If the writing teacher determines that students will complete a certain number of blog entries for the class, he or she would also have to determine which previous assignments or activities would be appropriate to jettison in order to make space for the new assignment. Sometimes this is easy because it may be that the digital assignment merely substitutes for a similar print assignment the teacher has had in place for years. Other times, though, it may not be so simple, since she would also need to ensure that what she omits does not result in unplanned loss of other outcomes or competencies. The writing teacher, for instance, might connect the blog entry to the following WPA Outcomes:

- Under Rhetorical Knowledge—focus on a purpose and adopt appropriate voice, tone, and level of formality
- Under Critical Thinking, Reading, and Writing—use writing and reading for inquiry, learning, thinking, and communicating and integrate their own ideas with those of others
- Under Processes—be aware that it takes multiple drafts to create and complete a successful text, understand the collaborative and social aspects of writing processes, and use a variety of technologies to address a range of audiences
- Under Knowledge of Conventions—develop knowledge of genre conventions ranging from structure and paragraphing to tone and mechanics

We could imagine that a teacher could determine some redundancy with this and other assignments or activities in the class to make room for such an activity. However, if he or she chose to give up an inquiry project to make room for the blog assignment because of overlap with the listed outcomes, he or she will have to consider which other outcomes might be lost that are not included in the hypertech assignment. In this case, the teacher might unintentionally lose outcomes around developing questions, investigating a problem, and conducting research. If he or she gives these up, it should be conscious and in consideration of the larger scope of class assignments and outcomes. Rather than looking at a single assignment and a set of outcomes, the writing teacher needs to have the larger framework of the course curriculum in mind, including the full spectrum of assignments and outcomes. If the hypertech fits within the framework of the larger curriculum and meets outcomes in a measurable way without compromising others, it would suggest that this particular implementation might be one to pursue. Technologies that are adopted without such consideration could result in detrimental effects for student writers coming through that course or program.

Part of the fear generated with new texts and technologies is either that (1) this new work will be in addition to the conventional work of writing, creating a course with so much content that it becomes impossible to teach well or (2) this new work will displace traditional efforts worth preserving that may not be achieved with the new hypertechs. If it were a simple one-to-one trade-off, the decision might be a bit simpler, but it is not. The larger picture of outcomes is worth carefully considering in terms of both its potential and its unintended consequences when introducing new technologies into the writing classroom.

Question 2: What obstacles or points of resistance need to be addressed or overcome to implement the technology?

Even if an assessor has a clear sense of the outcomes, it does not guarantee the successful implementation of the technology. Many a thoughtful assessment technology has failed or become less effective than its potential because of resistance or obstacles that stand between the plan and the experience. My mother, a first-generation American whose parents emigrated from Scotland to the United States in the early part of the 20th century, often cites the poet Robert Burns: "The best laid schemes o' Mice an' Men, gang aft agley." Technological implementations of hypertechs and their assessments are no exception to that proverb.

Obstacles take on a variety of forms, but I consider them to be non-human barriers to the implementation of the assessment technology. Access to the technology can be a barrier for many of us or our students. I remember first seeing Todd Taylor's work and being in awe of what he was doing with his students at the University of North Carolina, Chapel Hill. I also remember, though, thinking that the access he and his students had to digital technologies was significantly different from mine. His students had access to cameras, microphones, digital video editing software, and a variety of programs to manipulate and compose in hypermedia long before my students had such access. That did not mean that I could not venture down the path of hypermedia composing, but it did mean that I was not going as far or as quickly as I might have as long as my students lacked access to available technologies for such composition.

Another obstacle related to access is that of infrastructure. DeVoss, Cushman, and Grabill (2005) write about how their plans for classes in digital texts and technologies were thwarted by the lack of storage space their institution provided students to work on long-term digital texts. Many ePortfolio systems have run into problems with storage, retrieval, management, support, and troubleshooting with the infrastructure. The predicament is heightened when a program or institution wants to develop hypertechs on a large scale as opposed to a teacher looking for digital storage space for his or her students in only a few classes.

Obstacles often require partnerships and teamwork to overcome. Teachers and administrators often have our hands full with the work we are currently doing without adding an additional layer of collaboration and team building to our workloads. We also need to be aware of the obstacles, including ones that cannot be easily overcome with our current level of resources (funding, expertise, etc.). For example, one might not in one's current context feel ready to implement an open-source ePortfolio system if one doesn't have the technical support one might have at a different location. I've talked to several secondary teachers who would benefit from responding to networked blogs but cannot implement them because of restrictions on external Internet access. While there are internal systems to use within many of these schools districts, some teachers determine that they would be better off spending their time and energy on something else.

In addition to obstacles, human constraints can obstruct the implementation of new technologies through resistance from a number of sources. It can come from administrators or faculty from other disciplines who still consider the work of composition as service, preparing students for upper-level "content courses." If this is the assumption, they may not see composition work in the form of a video essay or a podcast as preparatory for writing in other classes. While this conflict may position us to engage them in dialogue with the goals and purposes of writing courses, in other situations it might not be beneficial to draw that type of negative attention to the class or program. An emerging trend over the past several years that I think is very helpful in relation to this resistance is the showcase events that many writing programs are now hosting (Purdue, Michigan State, and Florida State all host such events). Not only does it give students the opportunity to showcase their work and receive responses to it from real audiences, it provides a space for educators to converse about the work of hypertechs as related to writing courses, their outcomes, and connections to other segments of the institution.

Resistance can also come from within: from teachers or directors or administrators within our own departments and programs. These points of resistance may be more difficult to address than external resistance, since the insider has a disciplinary stake in the result as well. In some ways, we are used to being misunderstood by or misrepresented to others, but being targeted by those who are supposed to be allies or value our work can be more damaging. Part of the writing teacher's or administrator's role in hypertech writing and assessment is to continue ferreting out collaborative support, especially from those from within our programs, majors, and departments who understand and support the larger mission and vision of writing at our institutions.

Finally, and perhaps most seriously, resistance can come from students engaging with hypertechs and assessment technologies. Their discomfort may be derived from a variety of places, including their comfort zones, their goals, their experiences, and their connection to dominant cultural assumptions and narratives of technologies. While many students approach creative and experimental assignments with enthusiasm, others do not and their voices should not be silenced in this dialogue. Many of my upper-level students, who have been largely successful with their print-based literacies, find themselves in an unfamiliar place when presented with hypertech assignments and assessments. For many, this is disconcerting. After having been affirmed and receiving high marks with traditional assignments, who would blame them for feeling uncertain about a new type of literacy being thrown at them for the first time near the end of their educational experience? Students earlier in their college education are more willing to engage in experimental hypertechs, but they have concerns as well, including developing the rhetorical skills and knowledge to be successful in other composing situations in their college careers. I remember a student telling me that her high school teacher told her she needed to work on commas, and she wondered how the assignments in hypermedia would help her. It reminds me of Lisa Delpit's (1995) argument against process pedagogy, specifically how this new approach to teaching writing would disadvantage minority students who most needed traditional writing skills for college success (p. 45). While I have been challenged to think about this and other related concerns, I return to the outcomes and how there will be time and space for students to work on mechanics and correctness at this stage in the process and at other points in the semester.

In order to overcome obstacles and resistance to a writing curriculum that includes new texts and technologies and perhaps some new assessments besides, we can anticipate from where the resistance and obstacles will come. Who is it most critical to get "on board" with the new assignments or curriculum in order to overcome them? Building partnerships as we implement these new texts and assessment technologies can help ensure the maximum chance for their sustainability. Lone rangers can do only so much in this particular context and have only a limited influence on the larger community. Also important is time and scaling the implementation of digital texts and assessment technologies. My most common mistake is to get excited about some new writing or assessment technology and want to launch into it full scale immediately. Several of the best writing assessments have started small with pilots or just a few interested faculty. Further, some of the best writing courses have evolved over time and slowly grown into what is now a full-scale hypertech writing class. We know where we are and have a sense of where we would like to go. It is wiser to get there in a way that minimizes hardships that students, faculty, or administrators are bound to face in implementing a new writing or assessment technology.

Perhaps one of the most challenging obstacles we face in implementing new writing and assessment technologies in our writing classes is ourselves, specifically our lack of expertise and confidence in these new technologies that prevents us from allowing our students to explore new media literacy possibilities in their composing processes. This relates directly to the most common question I am asked when I talk about and present hypermedia composing to writing teachers. It begins with affirmation but ends in uncertainty: "I enjoyed the students' examples of new media writing, but how do you respond to and assess something like this? Do you have a rubric we could use?" So this is the subject of the last section of this chapter.

OLD FRAMEWORKS FOR NEW ASSESSMENTS

In order to determine which writing and assessment technologies to invest in and implement in our local contexts, we need consistent frameworks that help us examine and make consistent, meaningful choices in the technologies we develop and employ. Randomly integrating new technologies is no more desirable than uncritical acceptance or rejection of the technologies. Two such frameworks that provide access to such insights are unified construct validity and an examination of writing or educational outcomes in relation to the technology. In the former, a unified construct validity argument focuses our attention specifically on accuracy, the appropriateness, and social consequences of using certain results of assessment technologies to make educational decisions. Many newer digital writing assessments have not been processed through such a filter, since they are assumed to be acceptable simply because they are available, efficient, or objective. Validity arguments take time to measure, as they include multiple variables that are not always immediately apparent, and appropriateness is a long-term measure and must include unintended as well as intended consequences. The consequences of high-tech writing and assessment technologies are of particular interest because digital technologies tend to be sites of power, hegemony, and authority.

Outcomes are another framework through which educators can determine the suitability of hypertechs in relation to writing courses and programs. Certain hypertech applications readily correspond to existing outcomes, while others might push curriculum and pedagogy in directions that we are only beginning to understand. In either case merely matching an outcome with a hypertech does not fully satisfy the inquiry. Rather than move beyond outcomes, writing experts in the discipline need to consider revisiting outcomes in relation to hypertech writing in order to determine a more comprehensive vision of 21st-century literacies. Writing in the digital age is changing rapidly, and we must be vigilant to (re)consider new and existing student outcomes on a regular basis. University writing courses are often painfully disconnected from the writing in which students are engaged outside our sphere of influence. Likewise, many writing assessments are glaringly disconnected from the authentic writing students complete in class and in other contexts. In order to stay relevant and exert appropriate influence in matters of 21st-century literacy, writing experts in the discipline must consider how new assessment technologies need to respond to digital texts and technlogies.

The (R)evolution of Writing and Its Assessment

Every generation needs a new revolution.

—Thomas Jefferson

WHEN MY DAUGHTER was 6 years old, she came home from school one day clearly upset about something. When I asked about her day, she immediately informed me with some indignation that she needed to find a publisher for her new book, and she didn't know where to find one. I understood and sympathized with her concern (more than she knew). When I asked about the book, she proceeded to show me a three-chapter, 17-page book titled *The Magic Unicorn* that she had written and illustrated based on a story she and two friends made up during their time on the playground. Each page of writing had a corresponding illustration; the book had a cover page, title page, and chapter index; and the last page indicated that one of the unicorns in this book would be a recurring character in her next book. By the end of the week, she had finished the second book and already come up with the idea for a third book in what she then proudly called her trilogy. Being the curious and meddling father that I am, I asked her why she needed a publisher. She had a paper copy that we would save and read whenever she wanted. Those of us who have taught writing will not be surprised by her response. She wanted the book to be published not for tenure and promotion, not to protect her intellectual property, and not as a revenue source. She had written and illustrated these stories for an anticipated audience—primarily her extended family and friends who live around the country—and she pictured them reading and enjoying her work.

For my daughter the important parts of her creative processes included developing the ideas in collaboration with her friends, producing the text and developing visuals to communicate something of value to her, choosing the best materials to produce the book, and finding ways to distribute her writing to her audience of friends and family across the country. It is not surprising that many of these characteristics of her authentic writing context are foundational principles in the teaching of writing. What she completed could not be done within the confines of most current academic environments because it does not fit nicely into an educational box, and it is not particularly easy to assess and compare her work against others. How would we assess the collaboration? She developed the ideas with friends, but she was the one who inscribed and developed the ideas. How would we as writing teachers assess the visuals? They are an important part of the book, but we often feel unqualified to comment on and evaluate nonwritten modes of communication. Should the production of the book count? What about the page layout and design? What about her sense of audience? Did she have a clear sense of them and their expectations? The motivation, publication, and hypertechs she uses in this authentic writing event seem outside the comfort level and boundaries of how we normally teach and assess writing. And yet that is what hypertech writing and assessment is all about.

I was confronted by some of these same questions with Christine's multimodal essay on the role of satire in political cartoons. In assigning such a text, I was faced with the "problem" of assessing it, which was not such a problem at all. It was not a problem because we had talked about the criteria and expectations for the argument as well as the technology. The essay class had outcomes that were transferrable to the use of nonlinguistic texts, and she had completed a reflection to accompany the multimodal work in which she provided rationale for her decisions on the visuals and audio. Perhaps as important, though, was that I had the leeway within my institution and class to assign and teach such a text. Doing so did not take away valuable teaching time because how I taught this assignment was rhetorical in complimenting the content of the course. Experimental texts tend to take a bit longer than traditional essays, and many times technical glitches create frustrations for students. While I do not emphasize or grade the technological sophistication of the project, students often have a vision for what they want to do, and they have an audience beyond me as the teacher for whom they are composing. They upload their projects to a Web site such as YouTube or their portfolio, so much of their perfectionism is based on a real audience they envision and their investment in the final product.

Writing assessments should support and encourage the best practices possible in the teaching of writing and the best learning for our students, who are the in process of improving and building upon their literacy practices. While it might seem obvious that encouraging best practices in teaching and learning should be the primary goal of writing assessments, often these values get relegated to positions of lesser importance in the implementation of writing assessments. Other peripheral issues—political, social, financial, institutional, and statistical—often usurp the values of teaching and learning that writing assessments are supposed to promote.

Most notable about new media texts such as Christine's or my daughter's is that while they are high tech in their own right, they challenge the mechanistic direction in which educational assessment is currently moving. Les Perelman (2009) in his Conference on College Composition and Communication (CCCC) presentation "The Five-Paragraph Essay Makes People Stupid and Machines Smart" referred to the rumors that in 2015 the SAT Writing portion will be machine graded. He noted the compatibility between the five-paragraph essay and the way testing companies "manufacture construct validity." While testing companies are closing in on developing formulas to score highly conventional essays like the five-paragraph theme, imagine the difficulty of "counting" the effectiveness of a series of *New Yorker* cover images or a *Seinfeld* clip. The inability of machines to read—or of humans to read mechanistically—becomes even more pronounced when we add hypermediated texts to the equation (or algorithm in this case). So while I can evaluate and defend the use of new media texts within the context of my course outcomes and goals, they are quite a different burden for mechanized writing assessments. They require a type of reading and response that only a human reader can provide. Perhaps that is why they resonate so much for me.

Digital technologies are changing the writing and the texts we teach as well as how we respond to and evaluate them. I certainly have benefited from and taken advantage of the many newer digital technologies in my classes. In fact, I would claim that I am a better teacher (and writer, for that matter) than I would be without many of these digital technologies. However, we are intelligent enough and have enough teaching experience to know that the claims being made by those marketing or otherwise promoting the latest, greatest technologies will not live up to the hype. Regardless of the technology, students will still struggle with everything from grammar and mechanics to procrastinating on their writing assignments. At the same time we do not want to miss out on opportunities to support student learning and our writing programs.

One role we as writing experts can play is to encourage the most thoughtful and reflective explorations of new technologies that are being produced under the auspices of composition. While not all in the field agree that this exploration is the most healthy and productive way to proceed, others are quite convinced that we need to try as we might to keep up with current, cultural literacy practices, and that they should inform the ways in which we teach writing. Many of us have read or heard about the 21-year-old Japanese novelist named Rin, who, when she was a senior in high school, wrote a novel called *If You* that was originally produced and distributed via texting on cell phones. After her readers voted hers the best of the cell phone novels—an emerging genre that many are likening to graphic novels—in 2007, it was published in print and became the fifth-largest seller of the year, selling over 400,000 copies ("Thumbs," 2008). Many in rhetoric and composition, especially those who identify with new technologies, find this kind of emerging genre fascinating and worth exploring in classroom settings. Others find this appalling. Precisely because it is cutting edge and connected with a cell phone technology with which many students identify, writing classes could include an exploration of such new-media literacy. In response, logistical questions about access to phones and text messaging services arise, not to mention the questions about it and how it could be included in schools. I would venture to guess, though, that many of the most adventurous early adopters of technologies would respond by saying that they do not worry about assessment; their role is to push the boundaries and see what is possible, and they are ready to move on to the next challenge and let others worry about mundane tasks such as assessment.

That way of thinking represents at least two problems. First and most serious, writing assessment is often understood as separate and detached from teaching and learning. I would argue that is the case because those of us who are most interested in writing assessments have made it that way—a type of insider knowledge that revolves around psychometrics and statistics rather than students and their writing. Much of the current and best work in writing assessment has been doing just that, and while it may not be the dominant voice in assessment work, it is gaining important momentum. And second, without an element of appropriate assessment, it is difficult if not impossible to determine what if any effect—positive or negative—hypertechs are having on student writers.

It is not enough to merely critique the current state of writing assessment. Advocates for assessment argue that educators attempt to identify students as early as possible who do not have the skills necessary to achieve at higher levels so they can provide additional support to help them improve and succeed. I am reminded of an anecdote a writing program director told me of a student who came to her in tears after not passing a 1st-year writing portfolio. The student exclaimed, "[—— College] has failed me because I have not passed this portfolio," to which my friend replied, "No, it's quite the opposite. We have not failed you because we still have time to teach you and work with you on your writing before you graduate." This student is particularly fortunate because the writing assessment currently in place is consistent with many of the best practices in writing instruction and literacy learning (process, multiple writing samples, available workshops and tutoring, etc.). Not all students who are identified as "in need" from writing assessments get the same level of support and instruction.

The social and educational consequences of the way we are assessing student writing need to be considered in the larger debate as well. Too often the current writing assessments do not and cannot adequately measure writing as an engaged, communicative literacy event within current contextual constraints. What we know about good writing and response practices is being subsumed by the pragmatic concerns of testing mass populations for the purposes of comparison and sorting. It is not surprising that under the enormous pressure for accurate and appropriate information to which we look to make decisions about students and their writing, we have bought into the promises of technological solutions to social and educational problems. In our cultural understanding of technology, this is exactly its promise—that technological solutions are available that will allow us to continue down this mechanized path of testing. But many of the most widespread writing assessment technologies currently in use too often result in reductive, diminished views of writing and undermine our best efforts to deliver effective writing instruction and assessment.

Many of the current writing assessment technologies are aligned with values of efficiency, uniformity, speed, and mechanization. Some of these technologies are so deeply entrenched in educational contexts that they seem nearly impossible to challenge, and yet there are voices that have and continue to speak into these contexts. We have mistaken elevated uniformity and consistency for fairness, resulting in writing assessments that are inconsistent with many of the most fundamental values and best practices associated with the field. These current assessment models are bolstered by their strong connection to large-scale social, public perceptions of technological fixes and reductive views of literacy that tend to reduce language to surface features, formulaic arrangement, diminished writing processes, and social dynamics of written communication, and often function outside a rhetorical context for writing. These assessments allow us to manage and compare mass populations of students and perhaps reduce the "burden" of classroom assessments, but they fall short of more desirable outcomes.

But that's not to say that all new technologies in writing assessment are necessarily leading us down that path. There are those working against the cultural assumptions and narratives to develop and design assessment technologies that are locally controlled and managed. While they may be more costly and less efficient, many are resulting in localized assessments that provide students and educators with exactly the information they need to improve writing and the teaching of writing. They can respond, as well, to unique and individualized curricula and student needs.

If some writing assessment technologies are better than others, by what criteria do we measure them? One way is through the process of measuring validity. Because validity is measured, not as an either/or proposition, but rather as a level of degree, we can and should argue for them to support teaching. We can also assess our assessments by continuing our rich dialogue about the purposes of composition and what students should be able to know, think, and accomplish after taking our classes. Through student reflection and an examination of student-composed hypertechs, we can shape our classes into educational spaces that will promote 21st-century literacies. And by staying out ahead of the technological curve, we can insert our voices and ideas into the development of new writing and assessment technologies that will propel us in directions we are only beginning to imagine in the discipline.

Bibliography

American Educational Research Association, American Psychological Association, and National Council on Measurement in Education. (1985). *Standards of educational and psychological testing*. Washington, DC: Authors.

Anson, C. M. (2006). Can't touch this: Reflections on the servitude of computers as readers. In P. F. Ericsson & R. Haswell (Eds.), *Machine scoring of student essays: Truth and consequences* (pp. 38–56). Logan: Utah State University Press.

Aronowitz, S. (2000). *The knowledge factory: Dismantling the corporate university and creating true higher learning*. Boston: Beacon Press.

Ball, A. (1997). Expanding the dialogue on culture as a critical component when assessing writing. *Assessing Writing, 4*, 169–202.

Ball, C. E. (2004). Show, not tell: The value of new media scholarship. *Computers and Composition, 21*, 403–425.

Ball, C. E. (2006). Designerly ≠ readerly: Re-assessing multimodal and new media rubrics for writing studies. *Convergence: The International Journal for Research into New Media Technologies, 12*, 393–412.

Ball, C. E., & Kalmbach, J. (Eds.). (2010). *RAW: (Reading and writing) new media*. Cresskill, NJ: Hampton Press.

Baron, D. (1999). From pencils to pixels: The stages of literacy technologies. In G. E. Hawisher & C. L. Selfe (Eds.), *Passions, pedagogies, and 21st century technologies* (pp. 15–33). Logan: Utah State University Press.

Baron, D. (2009). *A better pencil: Readers, writers, and the digital revolution*. New York: Oxford University Press.

Bartholomae, D. (1996). What is composition and (if you know what that is) why do we teach it? In L. Z. Bloom, D. A. Daiker, & E. M. White (Eds.), *Composition in the twenty-first century: Crisis and change* (pp. 11–28). Carbondale: Southern Illinois University Press.

Barton, E. (1994). Interpreting the discourse of technology. In C. Selfe & S. Hilligoss (Eds.), *Literacy and technology: The complications of teaching and learning with technology* (pp. 56–75). New York: Modern Language Association Press.

Bean, J. C. (1983). Computerized word-processing as an aid to revision. *College Composition and Communication, 34*, 146–148.

Beason, L. (2001). Ethos and error: How business people react to errors. *College Composition and Communication, 53*, 33–64.

Bedore, P., & Rossen-Knill, D. F. (2004). Informed self-placement: Is a choice offered a choice received? *WPA: Writing Program Administration, 28*, 55–78.

Belanoff, P. (1994). Portfolios and literacy: Why? In L. Black, D. D. Baiker, J. Sommers, & G. Stygall (Eds.), *New directions in portfolio assessment* (pp. 13–39). Portsmouth, NH: Boynton/Cook.

Belanoff, P., & Dickson, M. (Eds.). (1991). *Portfolios*. Portmouth, NH: Boynton/Cook.

Belanoff, P., & Elbow, P. (1986). Using portfolios to increase collaboration and community in a writing program. *Writing Program Administrators, 9*, 27–40.

Berlak, H. (1992a). The need for a new science of assessment. In H. Berlak, F. M. Newmann, E. Adams, D. A. Archbald, T. Burgess, J. Raven, & T. A. Romberg (Eds.), *Toward a new science of educational testing and assessment* (pp. 1–21). Albany: State University of New York Press.

Berlak, H. (1992b). Toward the development of a new science of educational testing and assessment. In H. Berlak, F. M. Newmann, E. Adams, D. A. Archbald, T. Burgess, J. Raven, & T. A. Romberg (Eds.) *Toward a New Science of Educational Testing and Assessment* (pp. 181–206). Albany: State University of New York Press.

Bitzer, L. F. (1968). The rhetorical situation. *Philosophy and Rhetoric, 1*, 1–14.

Black, L., Helton, E., & Sommers, J. (1994). Connecting current research on authentic and performance assessment through portfolios. *Assessing Writing, 1*, 247–266.

Blakesley, D. (2002). Directed self-placement in the university. *WPA: Writing Program Administration, 25*, 9–39.

Bolter, J. D. (2008, May 23). *Opening writing spaces: Inscription and technology*. Keynote address given at the 2008 Computers and Writing Conference.

Borton, S. C., & Huot, B. (2007). Responding and assessing. In C. L. Selfe (Ed.), *Multimodal composition: Resources for teachers* (pp. 99–112). Cresskill, NJ: Hampton Press.

Brandt, D. (2001). *Literacy in American lives*. Cambridge: Cambridge University Press.

Bridwell, L., Nancarrow, P., & Ross, D. (1984). The writing process and the writing machine: Current research on word processors relevant to the teaching of composition. In R. Beach & L. Bridwell (Eds), *New directions in composition research* (pp. 381–398). New York: Guilford.

Broad, B. (2000). Pulling your hair out: Crises of standardization on communal writing assessment. *Research in the Teaching of English, 35*, 213–260.

Broad, B. (2003). *What we really value: Beyond rubrics in teaching and assessing writing*. Logan: Utah State University Press.

Broad, B. (2006). More work for teacher? Possible futures of teaching writing in the age of computerized writing assessment. In P. F. Ericsson & R. Haswell (Eds.), *Machine scoring of student essays: Truth and consequences* (pp. 221–233). Logan: Utah State University Press.

Broad, R. (1994). Portfolio scoring: A contradiction in terms. In L. Black, D. A. Daiker, & J. Sommers (Eds.), *New directions in portfolio assessment* (pp. 263–276). Portsmouth, NH: Boynton/Cook.

Burke, K. (1966). *Language as symbolic action: Essays on life, literature, and method*. Berkeley: University of California Press.

Callahan, S. (1995). Portfolio expectations: Possibilities and limits. *Assessing Writing, 2*, 117–156.

Camp, R. (1993). Changing the model for the direct assessment of writing. In M. M. Williamson & B. A. Huot (Eds.), *Validating holistic scoring for writing assessment: Theoretical and empirical foundations* (pp. 45–78). Cresskill, NJ: Hampton Press.

Cherry, R. D., & Meyer, P. R. (1993). Reliability issues in holistic assessment. In M. M. Williamson & B. A. Huot (Eds.), *Validating holistic scoring for writing assessment: Theoretical and empirical foundations* (pp. 109–141). Cresskill, NJ: Hampton Press.

Colby, R. S., & Colby, R. (2008). A pedagogy of play: Integrating computer games into the writing classroom. *Computers and Composition, 25*, 300–312.

Collier, R. (1983). The word processor and revision strategies. *College Composition and Communication, 34*, 149–55.

Condon, W. (1997). Building bridges, closing gaps: Using portfolios to reconstruct the academic community. In K. B. Yancey & I. Weiser (Eds.), *Situating portfolios: Four perspectives* (pp. 196–213). Logan: Utah State University Press.

Condon, W. (2006). Why less is not more: What we lose by letting a computer score writing samples. In P. F. Ericsson & R. Haswell (Eds.), *Machine scoring of student essays: Truth and consequences* (pp. 211–220). Logan: Utah State University Press.

Cowan, R. S. (1985). How the refrigerator got its hum. In D. MacKenzie & J. Wajcman (Eds.), *The social shaping of technology: How the refrigerator got its hum* (pp. 202–218). Philadelphia: Open University Press.

Cronbach, L. (1971). Test validation. In R. L. Thorndike (Ed.), *Educational measurement* (pp. 443–507). Washington, DC: American Council of Education.

Cronbach, L. (1989). Construct validation after 30 years. In R. L. Linn (Ed.), *Intelligence: Measurement, theory, and public policy* (pp. 147–171). Urbana: University of Illinois Press.

Cushman, E. (2004). Composing new media: Cultivating landscapes of the mind. *Kairos: Rhetoric, Technology, Pedagogy, 9*(1). Retrieved October 10, 2008, from http://english.ttu.edu/kairos/9.1/binder.html?http://www.msu.edu/%7Ecushmane/one/landscape.html

Darling-Hammond, L. (1994). Performance-based assessment and educational equity. *Harvard Educational Measurement: Issues and Practices, 13*, 5–30.

Delpit, L. (1995). *Other people's children: Cultural conflict in the classroom.* New York: The New York Press.

DeVoss, D. N., Cushman, E., & Grabill, J. T. (2005). Infrastructure and composing: The *when* of new-media writing. *College Composition and Communication, 57*, 14–44.

DeVoss, D., & Porter, J. E. (2006). Why Napster matters to writing: Filesharing as a new ethic of digital delivery. *Computers and Composition, 23*, 178–210.

Ericsson, P. F. (2006). The meaning of meaning: Is a paragraph more than an equation? In P. F. Ericsson & R. Haswell (Eds.), *Machine scoring of student essays: Truth and consequences* (pp. 28–37). Logan: Utah State University Press.

Fastest-growing demographic on Facebook: Women over 55. Inside Facebook.

(2009, February 1). Retrieved July 1, 2009, from http://www.insidefacebook. com/2009/02/02/fastest-growing-demographic-on-facebook-women-over-55/

Feenberg, A. (1991). *Critical theory of technology*. New York: Oxford University Press.

Fish, S. (1987). Anti-foundationalism, *Theory Hope*, and the teaching of composition. In C. Loeb & V. Lokke (Eds.), *The current criticism*. Bloomington: Indiana University Press.

Fish, S. (1989). *Doing what comes naturally: Change, rhetoric, and the practice of theory in literary and legal studies*. Durham: Duke University Press.

Fox, M. (1988). Notes from the battlefield: Towards a theory of why people write. *Language Arts, 65*, 112–125.

Garcia, G. E., & Pearson, P. D. (1994). Assessment and diversity. *Review of Research in Education, 20*, 337–391.

Gitelman, L. (2006). *Always already new: Media, history, and the data of culture*. Cambridge: MIT Press.

Gossett, K., Lamanna, C., Squier, J., & Walker, J. (2002). Continuing to mind the gap: Teaching image and text in new media spaces. *Karios: Rhetoric, Technology, Pedagogy, 7*(3). Retrieved August 1, 2007, from http://english.ttu.edu/ kairos/7.3/binder2.html?coverweb/Gossett/index.html

Green, L. (2002). *Communication, technology, and society*. London: SAGE.

Haas, C. (1996). *Writing technology: Studies of the materiality of literacy*. Mahwah, NJ: Lawrence Erlbaum Associates.

Hamp-Lyons, L. (2005). What is writing? What is "scholastic aptitude"? What are the consequences? SAT I Writing—a trip down memory lane. *Assessing Writing, 10*(3), 151–156.

Hamp-Lyons, L., & Condon, W. (1993). Questioning assumptions about portfolio-based assessment. *College Composition and Communication, 44*, 176–190.

Hanson, F. A. (1993). *Testing testing: Social consequences of the examined life*. Berkeley: University of California Press.

Harris, J. (1985). Student writers and word processing: A preliminary evaluation. *College Composition and Communication, 36*, 323–330.

Hartley, C., Schendel, E., & Neal, M. (1999). Writing (online) spaces: Composing webware with Perl. *Computers and Composition: An International Journal for Teachers of Writing, 16*, 359–370.

Haswell, R. H. (2006). Automatons and automated scoring: Drudges, black boxes, and dei ex machina. In P. F. Ericsson & R. Haswell (Eds.), *Machine scoring of student essays: Truth and consequences* (pp. 57–78), Logan: Utah State University Press.

Hayles, N. K. (2002). *Writing machines*. Cambridge: MIT Press.

Hayles, N. K. (2007). Hyper and deep attention: The generational divide in cognitive modes. In *Profession 2007* (pp. 187–199). New York: Modern Language Association.

Heidegger, M. (1977). *The question concerning technology*. New York: Harper & Row.

Herrington, A., Hodgson, K., & Moran, C. (Eds.). (2009). *Teaching the new writing: Technology, change, and assessment in the 21st century classroom*. New York: Teachers College Press.

Herrington, A., & Moran, C. (2001). What happens when machines read our students' writing? *College English, 63,* 480–499.

Herrington, A., & Moran, C. (2006). WritePlacer Plus in place: An exploratory case study. In P. F. Ericsson & R. Haswell (Eds.), *Machine scoring of student essays: Truth and consequences* (pp. 114–129). Logan: Utah State University Press.

Hillocks, G. (1995). *Teaching writing as reflective practice.* New York: Teachers College Press.

Houle, B. R., Kimball, A. P., & McKee, H. A. (2005). Boy? girl? you decide: Multimodal Web composition and a mythography of identity. *Computers and Composition Online.* Retrieved August 1, 2007, from http://www.bgsu.edu/cconline/houlekimballmckee/index.html

Howard, R. M. (2007). Understanding Internet plagiarism. *Computers and Composition, 24,* 3–15.

Huot, B. A. (1990). Reliability, validity, and holistic scoring: What we know and what we need to know. *College Composition and Communication, 41,* 201–213.

Huot, B. A. (1993). The influence of holistic scoring procedures on reading and rating student essays. In M. M. Williamson & B. A. Huot (Eds.), *Validating holistic scoring for writing assessment: Theoretical and empirical foundations* (pp. 206–236). Cresskill, NJ: Hampton Press.

Huot, B. A. (1996a). Computers and assessment: Understanding two technologies. *Computers and Composition, 13,* 231–243.

Huot, B. A. (1996b). Toward a new theory of assessment. *College Composition and Communication, 47,* 549–566.

Huot, B. A. (2002). *(Re)articulating writing assessment.* Logan: Utah State University Press.

Huot, B. A., & Neal, M. R. (2006). Writing assessment: A techno-history. In C. A. MacArthur, S. Graham, & J. Fitzgerald (Eds.), *Handbook of writing research,* (pp. 417–432). New York: Guilford Press.

Huot, B. A., & Williamson, M. M. (1997). Rethinking portfolios for evaluating writing: Issues of assessment and power. In K. B. Yancey & I. Weiser (Eds.), *Situating portfolios: Four perspectives* (pp. 43–56). Logan: Utah State University Press.

Jacobsen, J. (2000). *Technical fouls: Democratic dilemmas and technological change.* Boulder, CO: Westview Press.

Jencks, C. (1998). Racial bias in testing. In C. Jencks & M. Phillips (Eds.), *The black-white test score gap* (pp. 55–85). Washington, DC: Brookings Institution Press.

Jencks, C., & Phillips, M. (Eds.). (1998). *The Black-White test score gap.* Washington, DC: Brookings Institution Press.

Johnson-Eilola, J., & Selber, S. A. (2007). Plagiarism, originality, assemblage. *Computers and Composition, 24,* 375–403.

Jones, E. (2006). ACCUPLACER's essay-scoring technology: When reliability does not equal validity. In P. F. Ericsson & R. Haswell (Eds.), *Machine scoring of student essays* (pp. 93–113). Logan: Utah State University Press.

Jones, S. (2006). *Against technology: From the Luddites to neo-Luddism.* New York: Routledge.

Kameen, P. (2000). *Writing/teaching: Essays toward a rhetoric of pedagogy.* Pittsburgh: University of Pittsburgh Press.

Knieval, M. (2009). What is humanistic about computers and writing? Historical patterns and contemporary possibilities for the field. *Computers and Composition, 26,* 92–106.

Kobrin, J. L., Patterson, B. F., Shaw, E. J., Mattern, K. D., & Barbuti, S. M. (2008). *Validity of the SAT for predicting first-year college grade point average.* Retrieved December 20, 2009, from http://professionals.collegeboard.com/profdownload/pdf/08–1718_RDRR_081017_Web.pdf

Landow, G. P. (1997). *Hypertext 2.0: The convergence of contemporary critical theory and technology.* Baltimore: Johns Hopkins University Press.

Lemann, N. (1999). *The big test: The secret history of the American meritocracy.* New York: Farrar, Straus, & Giroux.

Lewiecki-Wilson, C., Sommers, J., & and Tassoni, J. P. (2000). Rhetoric and the writer's profile: Problematizing directed self-placement. *Assessing Writing, 7,* 165–183.

Liptak, A. (2009, June 29). Supreme Court finds bias against White firefighters. *The New York Times Online.* Retrieved July 20, 2009, from http://www.nytimes.com/2009/06/30/us/30scotus.html?_r=1

Lunsford, A. (2006). Writing, technologies, and the fifth canon. *Computers and Composition, 23,* 169–177.

Lyotard, J. F. (1979). *The postmodern condition: A report on knowledge.* Manchester: Manchester University Press, 1984.

MacKenzie, D., & Wajcman, J. (Eds.). (1985). *The social shaping of technology.* Buckingham: Open University Press.

Madaus, G. (1993). A national testing system: Manna from above? An historical/technological perspective. *Educational Measurement, 11,* 9–26.

Madaus, G. (1994). A technological and historical consideration of equity issues associated with proposals to change the nation's testing policy. *Harvard Educational Review, 64,* 76–95.

Manovich, L. (2001). *The language of new media.* Cambridge: MIT Press.

McGee, T. (2006). Taking a spin on the intelligent essay assessor. In P. F. Ericsson & R. Haswell (Eds.), *Machine scoring of student essays: Truth and consequences,* (pp. 93–113). Logan: Utah State University Press.

Mensh, E., & Mensh, H. (1991). *The IQ mythology.* Carbondale: Southern Illinois University Press.

Mercer, J. R. (1989). Alternative paradigms for assessment in a pluralistic society. In J. Banks & C. M. Banks (Eds.), *Multicultural Education* (pp. 289–303). Boston: Allyn & Bacon.

Messick, S. (1989). Meaning and values in test validation: The science and ethics of assessment. *Educational Researcher, 18,* 5–12.

Mesthene, E. G. (1970). *Technological change: Its impact on man and society.* Cambridge: Harvard University Press.

Moss, P. A. (1992). Shifting conceptions of validity in educational measurement: Implications for performance assessment. *Review of Educational Research, 62,* 229–258.

Moss, P. A. (1994). Can there be validity without reliability? *Educational Researcher, 23,* 5–12.

Moss, P. A. (1998). Testing the test of the test: A response to multiple inquiry in the validation of writing tests. *Assessing Writing, 5,* 111–122.

Murphy, S. (1997). Teachers and students: Reclaiming assessment via portfolios. In K. B. Yancey & I. Weiser (Eds.), *Situating portfolios: Four perspectives.* Logan: Utah State University Press.

Murphy, S., & Grant, B. (1996). Portfolio approaches to assessment: Breakthrough or more of the same. In E. M. White, W. D. Lutz, & S. Kamusikiri (Eds.), *Assessment of writing: Politics, policies, practices.* New York: Modern Language Association.

Murray, J. (2009). *Non-discursive rhetoric: Image and affect in multimodal composition.* Albany: State University of New York Press.

New London Group. (1996). A pedagogy of multiliteracies: Designing social futures. *Harvard Educational Review, 66,* 60–92.

Norbert, E. (2005). *On a scale: A social history of writing assessment in America.* New York: Peter Lang.

Nye, D. E. (2004). Technological prediction: A Promethean problem. In M. Sturken, D. Thomas, & S. J. Ball-Rokeach (Eds.), *Technological visions: The hopes and fears that shape new technologies* (pp. 159–176). Philadelphia: Temple University Press.

Official SAT Practice Test 2008–2009. Retrieved July 5, 2009, from http://www.scribd.com/doc/16311030/Official-SAT-Practice-Test-20082009

Oliver, S. (1994). Anticipating tomorrow: Technology and the future. In L. Green & R. Guinery (Eds.), *Framing technology: Society, choice and change* (pp. 45–59). Sydney: Allen & Unwin.

Pearson, B. Z. (2005). Predictive validity of the scholastic aptitude test (SAT) for Hispanic bilingual students. *Hispanic Journal of Behavioral Sciences, 15*(3), 342–356.

Penrod, D. (2005). *Composition in convergence: The impact of new media on writing assessment.* Mahwah, NJ: Lawrence Erlbaum.

Perelman, L. (2009, March 12). *The five-paragraph essay makes people stupid and machines smart.* Paper presented at the annual Conference on College Composition and Communication. San Francisco.

Prensky, M. (2001). Digital natives, digital immigrants. *On the Horizon, 9,* 1–2.

Reynolds, N. (2000). *Portfolio teaching: A guide for instructors* (1st ed.). Boston: Bedford/St. Martin's Press.

Rice, J. (2003). Writing about cool: Teaching hypertext as juxtaposition. *Computers and Composition, 19,* 221–236.

Rife, M. C. (2007). The fair use doctrine: History, application, and implications for (new media) writing teachers. *Computers and Composition, 24,* 154–178.

Royer, D. J., & Gilles, R. (1998). Directed self-placement: An attitude of orientation. *College Composition and Communication, 50,* 54–70.

Royer, D. J., & Gilles, R. (Eds.). (2003). *Directed self-placement: Principles and practices.* Cresskill, N. J.: Hampton Press.

Scharton, M. (1996). The politics of validity. In E. M. White, W. D. Lutz, & S. Kamusikiri (Eds.), *Assessment of Writing: Politics, Policies, Practices* (pp. 52–75). New York: Modern Language Association.

Schendel, E., & O'Neill, P. (1999). Exploring the theories and consequences of self-assessment through ethical inquiry. *Assessing Writing, 6,* 199–227.

Schneiderman, R. (2003). *Technology lost: Hype of reality in the digital age.* Upper Saddle River, NJ: Prentice Hall.

Selber, S. A. (2004). *Multiliteracies for a digital age.* Carbondale: Southern Illinois University Press.

Selfe, C. L. (1999). *Technology and literacy in the 21st century: The importance of paying attention.* Carbondale: Southern Illinois University Press.

Selfe, C. L. (2004). Students who teach us: A case study of a new media text designer. In A. F. Wysocki, J. Johnson-Eilola, C. L. Selfe, & G. Sirc (Eds.), *Writing new media: Theory and applications for expanding the teaching of composition* (pp. 43–66). Logan: Utah State University Press.

Selfe, C. A. (Ed.). (2008). *Multimodal composition: Resources for teachers.* Cresskill, NJ: Hampton Press.

Shallis, M. (1984). *The silicon idol: The micro revolution and its social implications.* Oxford: Oxford University Press.

Shepard, L. (1993). Evaluating test validity. *Review of Research in Education, 19,* 405–450.

Shepard, L. (1995). Using assessment to improve learning. *Educational Leadership, 52,* 38–43.

Shepard, L. (1997). The centrality of test use and consequences for test validity. *Educational Measurement: Issues and Practice, 16,* 5–24.

Sheppard, J. (2009). The rhetorical work of multimedia production practices: It's more than just technical skill. *Computers and Composition, 26,* 122–131.

Smith, J. B., & Yancey, K. B. (Eds.). (2000). *Self-assessment and development in writing: A collaborative inquiry.* Cresskill, NJ: Hampton Press.

Smith, W. L. (1993). Assessing the reliability of adequacy of using holistic scoring of essays as a college composition placement technique. In B. A. Huot & M. M. Williamson (Eds.), *Validating holistic scoring for writing assessment: Theoretical and empirical foundations* (pp. 142–205). Cresskill, NJ: Hampton Press.

Sommers, J. (1991). Bring practice in line with theory: Using portfolio grading in the composition classroom. In P. Belanoff & M. Dickson (Eds.), *Portfolios: Process and product* (pp. 153–164). Portsmouth, NH: Boynton/Cook.

Sorapure, M. (2006). Between modes: Assessing student new media compositions. *Kairos: Rhetoric, Technology, Pedagogy, 10*(2). Retrieved October 10, 2008, from http://english.ttu.edu/KAIROS/10.2/binder2.html?coverweb/sorapure/index.html

Stroupe, C. (2000). Visualizing English: Recognizing the hybrid literacy of visual and verbal authorship on the Web. *College English, 62,* 607–32.

Stroupe, C. (2007). Hacking the cool: The shape of writing culture in the space of new media. *Computers and Composition, 24,* 421–442.

Sturken, M., & Thomas, D. (2004). Technological visions and the rhetoric of the new. In M. Sturken, D. Thomas, & S. J. Ball-Rokeach (Eds.), *Technological visions: The hopes and fears that shape new technologies* (pp. 1–18). Philadelphia: Temple University Press.

Sturken, M., Thomas, D., & Ball-Rokeach, S. J. (Eds.). (2004). *Technological visions:*

The hopes and fears that shape new technologies. Philadelphia: Temple University Press.

Sudol, R. (1985). Applied word processing: Notes on authority, responsibility, and revision in a workshop model. *College Composition and Communication, 36,* 331–335.

Szymanski, N. (2010, March). *Understanding the journals that write us: Exploring the relationship between the field of composition and the subdiscipline of computers and composition.* Presented at the Conference on College Composition and Communication.

Takayoski, P. (1996). The shape of electronic writing: Evaluating and assessing computer-assisted writing processes and products. *Computers and Composition, 13,* 245–258.

Tardy, C. M. (2005). Expressions of disciplinarity and individuality in a multimodal genre. *Computers and Composition, 22,* 319–336.

Taylor, T. W. (2008). *Take 20.* Boston: Bedford/St. Martins.

Thumbs race as Japan's best sellers go cellular. (2008, January 20). *New York Times Online.* Retrieved March 1, 2009, from http://www.nytimes.com/2008/01/20/world/asia/20japan.html?_r=1

Turkle, S. (2004). "Spinning" technology: What we are not thinking about when we are thinking about computers. In S. Ball-Rokeach, M. Sturken, & D. Thomas (Eds.), *Technological visions: The hopes and fears that shape new technologies* (pp. 19–33). Philadelphia: Temple University Press.

Vie, S. (2008). Digital divide 2.0: "Generation M" and online social networking sites in the composition classroom. *Computers and Composition, 25,* 9–23.

Volti, R. (2001). *Society and technological change* (4th ed.). New York: Worth.

Westrum, R. (1991). *Technologies and society: The shaping of people and things.* Belmont, CA: Wadsworth.

White, E. M. (1985). Holisticism. *College Composition and Communication, 35,* 400–409.

White, E. M. (1993). Holistic scoring: Past triumphs, future challenges. In M. M. Williamson & B. A. Huot (Eds.), *Validating holistic scoring for writing assessment: Theoretical and empirical foundations* (pp. 79–108). Cresskill, NJ: Hampton Press.

Whithaus, C. (2005). *Teaching and evaluating writing in the age of computers and high stakes testing.* Mahwah, NJ: Lawrence Erlbaum.

Whithaus, C. (2006). Always already: Automated essay scoring and grammar-checkers in college writing courses. In P. F. Ericsson & R. Haswell (Eds.), *Machine scoring of student essays: Truth and consequences* (pp. 166–176). Logan, UT: Utah State University Press.

Wiggins, G. P. (1992). Creating tests worth taking. *Educational Leadership, 49*(8), 26–33.

Williamson, M. M. (1993). An introduction to holistic scoring: The social, historical, and theoretical context for writing assessment. In M. M. Williamson & B. A. Huot (Eds.), *Validating holistic scoring for writing assessment: Theoretical and empirical foundations* (pp. 1–44). Cresskill, NJ: Hampton Press.

Williamson, M. M. (1994). The worship of efficiency: Untangling theoretical and practical considerations in writing assessment. *Assessing Writing, 1,* 147–174.

Winner, L. (1985). *The social shaping of technology* (2nd ed.). Buckingham: Open University Press.

Winner, L. (2004). Sow's ear from silk purses: The strange alchemy of technological visions. In M. Sturken, D. Thomas, & S. J. Ball-Rokeach (Eds.), *Technological visions: The hopes and fears that shape new technologies* (pp. 34–47). Philadelphia: Temple University Press.

Wohlpart, A. J., Lindsey, C., & Rademacher, C. (2008). The reliability of computer software to score essays: Innovations in a humanities course. *Computers and Composition, 25*, 203–223.

Wysocki, A. F. (2004). Opening new media to writing: Openings and justifications. In A. F. Wysocki, J. Johnson-Eilola, C. L. Selfe, & G. Sirc (Eds.), *Writing new media: Theory and applications for expanding the teaching of composition,* (pp. 1–42), Logan, UT: Utah State University Press.

Wysocki, A. F., Johnson-Eilola, J., Selfe, C. L, & Sirc, G. (Eds.). (2004). *Writing new media: Theory and applications for expanding the teaching of composition.* Logan: Utah State University Press.

Yancey, K. B. (Ed.). (1992). *Portfolios in the writing classroom: An introduction.* Urbana, IL: National Council of Teachers of English.

Yancey, K. B. (1996a). Portfolio, electronic, and the links between. *Computers and Composition, 13*, 129–134.

Yancey, K. B. (1996b). Portfolio as genre, rhetoric as reflection: Situating selves, literacies, and knowledge. *WPA: Writing Program Administration, 19*, 55–69.

Yancey, K. B. (1998). *Reflection in the writing classroom.* Logan: Utah State University Press.

Yancey, K. B. (1999). Looking back as we look forward: Historicizing writing assessment. *College Composition and Communication, 50*, 483–503.

Yancey, K. B. (2001). Digitized student portfolios. In B. L. Cambridge (Ed.), *Electronic portfolios: Emerging practices in student, faculty, and institutional learning* (pp. 15–30). Washington, DC: American Association for Higher Education 15–30.

Yancey, K. B. (2004a). Made not only in words: Composition in a new key. *College Composition and Communication, 56*, 297–328.

Yancey, K. B. (2004b). Postmodernism, palimpsest, and portfolios: Theoretical issues in the representation of student work. *College Composition and Communication, 55*, 738–761.

Yancey, K. B., & Weiser, I. (1997). Situating portfolios: An introduction. In K. B. Yancey & I. Weiser (Eds.), *Situating portfolios: Four perspectives* (pp. 1–20). Logan: Utah State University Press.

Index

Accountability systems
  in accreditation, 30
  responsibility model as alternative to, 30
  statewide assessments, 17
  teachers and, 42, 44
Accreditation, accountability systems in, 30
ACCUPLACER, 72–73
Advanced placement (AP) test, 40, 64
AK-47 raffle, as ideological, 21–22
American Educational Research Association (AERA), 110
American Psychological Association (APA), 110, 111
Antidominant view of technology (Barton), 35–36
Aronowitz, Stanley, 37
Ask Jeeves, 24
Assumptions of writing assessments, 8–9, 15–32
  accountability through statewide assessments, 17
  cultural issues, 17–18
  determinism, 17–32
  instrumentalism, 17, 18–23, 31–32, 55–56, 132
  integral nature of digital texts and technologies, 16–17
  technological change, 15–16
  technological sociology in, 15
  transparency of writing assessments as technologies, 27–31
Audience analysis, 24
Audio/visual technologies, 76

Ball, Cheryl E., 2, 11, 94–95, 120
Barbuti, S. M., 38–39
Baron, Dennis, 17, 28
Bartholomae, David, 78
Barton, Ellen, 34, 35

Bean, J. C., 27
Beason, Larry, 73
Bedore, P., 28
Belanoff, Pat, 35–36, 79
Berlak, Herald, 114–115
Betamax platform, 51
Better Pencil, A (Baron), 17
Bitzer, Lloyd F., 74
Black, L., 79
Blakesley, D., 28
Blogs, 16, 76, 77–78, 93, 108
Blue Ray platform, 51
Bolter, Jay David, 48, 79, 102
Brain Age II, 101–102
Brandt, Deborah, 16, 54–55, 77, 100
Bridge design, as ideological, 21
Bridwell, L., 27
Broad, Robert, 61, 62, 64, 73, 79, 85, 95, 109, 117
Burke, K., 45
Burns, Robert, 123

Callahan, S., 80
Camp, R., 61, 62, 119
Cell phone novels, 130–131
Central Piedmont Community College, 90
Change
  as assumption of writing assessments as technology, 15–16
  instability faced by students and teachers, 16
Cherry, R. D., 110–111
Colby, R., 2
Colby, R. S., 2
College Board, 22, 43, 68–69
College Composition and Communication (journal), 28, 35, 73
College writing, problems of, 42
Collier, R., 27
COMPASS test, 25, 51–52

Composing
  technologies, 28
  writing versus, 92–93
Computers and Composition (journal), 35
Computers and writing, 48
Computer-scored writing, *See* Machine-
  scored student writing
Condon, William, 63, 67–68, 79
Conference on College Composition and
  Communication (CCCC; National
  Council of Teachers of English), 35, 48,
  111, 130
Consciousness, new media and, 92
Construct validity, 109–120, 126–127
  features of, 110
  manufacturing by test companies, 130
  unified, 112–120
Content bias, 39
Content validity, 110
Context
  educational, 20–21
  social, 20–21, 132
  in writing assessment with technology,
    12
Copyright, 2
Course management systems, 25, 26, 43–44,
  83
Criteria mapping methodology, 63, 85
Criterion-related validity, 110
Critical theory, 35–36
Cronbach, L., 109, 112
Cultural literacy practices, 130–131
Cultural narratives, 33–41
  balanced approach to technology, 41
  cultural metanarratives/grand narratives,
    33–34
  technophobia, 37–41
  technotopic narratives, 34–37
Culture, 6–7, 17–18
Cushman, Ellen, 2, 11, 124

Darling-Hammond, L., 22–23
Data mining, 82–83
del.icio.us, 76
Delpit, Lisa, 125
Design, and new assessment technologies,
  53–55, 83
Determinism
  active adoption of technology, 25
  humanization of technologies, 24

moving beyond, 31–32
nature of, 23
of new assessment technologies, 56
technological failure and, 26–27
technological imperative and, 24–25
technological invisibility and, 17, 23–27,
  29–30
transparency of writing assessments as
  technologies, 27
ubiquity of technology, 25–26
DeVoss, D. N., 2, 124
Dickson, M., 79
Digital alarm clocks, 25–26
Digital audio, 108
Digital editing programs, 108
Digital natives (Prensky), 28
Digital texts
  holistic scoring, 10, 17, 29, 36, 63–65,
    95–96
  machine-scored writing, 17, 65–75
  newest forms, 17
  types, 2-3, 10–11, 16, 76–78, 93, 108
  in writing assessment as technology, 16–17
  in writing assessment with technology,
    10–12
Digital video, 16, 76, 93, 108
Diigo, 76
Directed self-placement (DSP), 20, 28–29, 36
Discrimination
  gendered, 23, 38–39, 40, 119
  racial, 23, 38–39, 40
Discussion boards, 108
DVD platform, 51
Dynamic criteria mapping (DCM), 63, 85

Early adopters of new technologies, 45–46,
  56
Educational Testing Service (ETS), 22–23,
  37, 49, 51, 61, 62–63, 68
Efficiency in writing assessment, 36–37, 75
Elbow, P., 35
Electronic comments, 108
Electronic portfolios (ePortfolios), 5, 10–11,
  35–37, 43–44, 50–52, 55, 60, 79, 81–86
  connections in, 81, 90–91
  ePortfolio model at small private
    institution, 84–86
  evolution of, 78–86
  first-year composition (FYC) model,
    82–84

nature of, 81
print portfolios versus, 79–81
E-mail, 78, 108
ePortfolio systems, *See* Electronic portfolios (ePortfolios)
E-rater, 68
Ericsson, Patricia Freitag, 69–70
Essay-prompt composition, instrumentalism of technology and, 20
Essay-scoring software, 69–70, 72–73
Experts in writing, *See* Writing experts

Facebook, 76, 107
File sharing, 108
Firefox, 24
Fish, Stanley, 34
Flickr, 76
Florida, Sunshine State Standards, 4
Florida State University, 124
Formative assessment, 55
Fox, Mem, 71
Furlong, Edward, 76

Garcia, G. E., 22–23, 40
Gates, Bill, 106
Gendered discrimination, 23, 38–39, 40, 119
Gilles, R., 28
Ginsburg, Ruth Bader, 118–119
Grabill, J. T., 2, 124
Grading systems, 29–30, 68–69
rubrics, 10, 62–63, 83, 95–96, 113
Graduate Management Admissions Test (GMAT), 68
Grand narratives, 33–34
Grant, B., 36, 80
Graphic novels, 131
Green, L., 18
Gun raffle, as ideological, 21–22

Haas, Christina, 18, 21, 25, 30
Hamp-Lyons, L., 79
Hanson, F. A., 46
Harris, J., 27
Hartley, C., 53
Haswell, R. H., 66–67
Hayles, N. Katherine, 11, 67, 99–102
Heath, Shirley Brice, 100
Heidegger, M., 21
Helton, E., 79
Herrington, Anne, 66–69, 71

High-stakes writing assignments, 40, 43, 118
Hillocks, George, 38, 100
Holistic scoring, 10, 17, 29, 36, 63–65, 95–96
Houle, B. R., 77
Howard, R. M., 2
HTML coding, 101
Huot, Brian A., 7, 18, 30, 46, 54, 60, 61, 68, 69, 109, 115
Hybrid text, 102–103
Hyperactive hypertechs, 76–127
assessment issues, 86–91, 96–99, 103–104, 106–127
construct validity, 109–120, 126–127, 130
hyperattention, 10–11, 99–105
hypermedia, 10–11, 48, 78–79, 91–99, 104–105
hypertext, 10–11, 48, 78–91, 104–105
types of digital technologies, 76–78, 93, 108
writing outcomes, 109, 120–126, 127
Hyperattention, 10–11, 99–105
defined, 99, 100–101
hybrid text and, 102–103
implications for assessment, 103
implications for writing class, 103–104
nature of, 99
problems of, 99–100
in processing multiple information streams, 101–102
Hypermedia, 10–11, 48, 91–99, 104–105
classification systems, 91–92
defined, 92
developing reductive grading rubrics, 95–96
hypertext versus, 78–79
importing criteria from other disciplines, 95
key assessment criteria using, 96–99
as key textual revolution, 92–93
nature of, 91
pervasiveness of, 93
treating same as print texts, 94–95
Hypertext, 10–11, 48, 78–91, 104–105
assessing, 86–91
classroom-based print portfolios versus, 79–82
defined, 78
evolution of electronic portfolios, 78–86

Hypertext (*continued*)
hypermedia versus, 78–79
linked texts, 79–81

Implementation, of new assessment
technologies, 44–46, 121–126
Instant messaging, 78
Instrumentalism
directed self-placement (DSP), 20, 28–29, 36
goal for educators, 19
mass marketing of writing assessments,
19–20
moving beyond, 31–32
nature of, 18–19
of new assessment technologies, 55–56
problem of, 19
social and educational contexts of
technology, 20–21, 132
technological neutrality and, 17, 18–23
transparency of writing assessments as
technologies, 27
Intelligent Essay Assessor (IEA), 69–70, 72
IntelliMetric, 68, 70
Internet, 52
Interrater reliability, 115–117
Invisibility, technological determinism and,
17, 23–27, 29–30
iPod, 34–35
IUPUI, Office of Service Learning, 89–90

Jefferson, Thomas, 128
Jencks, C., 39, 40
Jobs, Steve, 34
Johnson-Eilola, J., 2
Jones, Edmund, 10, 71–73
Jones, S., 40–41

Kairos: A Journal of Rhetoric, 79
Kalmbach, J., 2
Kameen, Paul, 78
Kimball, A. P., 77
Knowledge Analysis Technologies, 69
Kobrin, J. L., 38–39

Label bias, 39
Landow, George P., 78
Lewiecki-Wilson, C., 28
Lindsey, C., 10
Listservs, 108
Luddites, 40–41
Lyotard, J. F., 33

Machine-scored student writing, 65–75
benefits of, 66
coding of text, 67–68
computer grading systems, 17, 68–70
essay-scoring software, 69–70, 72–73
misdirection of mechanization, 74–75
rationale for using, 66–67
trend toward, 65–70
writing experts and, 70–74
Macintosh platform, 51
MacKenzie, Donald, 8
Madaus, G., 7–8, 18, 22–23, 34
Manovich, Lev, 91, 93
Mattern, K. D., 38–39
McGee, Tim, 71, 72
McKee, H. A., 77
Mechanization process in writing
assessment, 9–10, 59–75
human-based assessment versus, 61, 113,
117
indirect versus direct measures of
writing, 61–65, 68
machine-scored student writing, 17, 60,
65–75
misdirection of mechanization, 74–75
plagiarism-detection programs, 25, 43–44,
50, 52, 60, 66, 93–94
reliability and, 115–116
trend toward, 60–70
Mensh, E., 119
Mensh, H., 119
Mercedes Benz Company, 47
Mercer, J. R., 22–23, 119
Messick, Samuel, 109, 112, 119
Methodological bias, 39–40
Meyer, P. R., 110–111
Michigan State University, 124
Microsoft, 15–16
Microsoft Word, 65–66
Monument/memorial re-design project, 45
Moran, Charles, 66–69, 71
Moss, Beverly, 100
Moss, Pamela A., 61, 77, 109, 113, 115, 119
Multimodal composition, hypermedia texts
as, 11
Multiple-choice tests, 39–40, 61, 118
Multiplicity of forms in hybrid expression
(Bolter), 102–103
Murphy, S., 35, 36, 80
Murray, Jody, 86, 89
MySpace, 76

Nancarrow, P., 27
National Council of Teachers of English (NCTE)
Conference on College Composition and Communication (CCCC), 35, 48, 111, 130
NCTE Read, Write, Think, 90
National Council on Measurement in Education, 110
NCTE Read, Write, Think, 90
Neal, M. R., 46, 53, 54
Negative narratives of writing assessment
relinquishing control of decision making, 40–41
technophobia, 37–41
test bias, 23, 38–40
Neo-Luddites, 41, 67
New assessment technologies, 42–56
choice of media and technology platforms, 45–46
course management systems, 25, 26, 43–44, 83
design, 53–55, 83
disciplinary investment in teaching of writing, 54–55
early adoption of, 45–46, 56
electronic portfolios (ePortfolios), 5, 10–11, 35–37, 43–44, 50–52, 55, 60, 79, 81–86
implementation, 44–46, 121–126
old frameworks for new assessments, 126–127
plagiarism-detection programs, 25, 43–44, 50, 52, 60, 66, 93–94
prediction, 46–52
problems of, 42–43
propositions concerning, 48–52
resistance to, 40–41, 56, 124–125
sponsorship of, 54–55
technician roles in developing, 42–43, 53
unintended consequences of, 37–38, 55–56, 118–120
writing expert roles in developing, 41, 43, 53–55, 70–74
New literacies, 2–3
New London Group, 91–92
New media
challenges of assessing, 11
hypermedia texts as, 10–11, 130
mathematical and linguistic nature of texts, 93–94

nature of, 1–2
new consciousness/awareness and, 92
types of, 2–3, 10–11, 16, 76–78, 93, 108
New Media Writing (Wysocki), 94
Nintendo DS Brain Age II, 101–102
No Child Left Behind, 7, 42
Norbert, E., 46
Nye, David E., 34, 48, 49, 51

Obama, Barack, 1, 108
Obama, Michelle, 1
Oliver, Susan, 47
O'Neill, P., 28

Page, Ellis, 68
Patterson, B. F., 38–39
Paulus, Dieter, 68
PC platform, 51
Pearson, P. D., 22–23, 40
Pen-and-paper composition
instrumentalism of technology and, 20
as nontechnology option, 28
Penrod, D., 109
Perelman, Les, 130
Phonograph, 52
Plagiarism, 2
Plagiarism-detection software, 25, 43–44, 50, 52, 60, 66, 93–94
Podcasts, 16, 93
Porter, J. E., 2
Portfolio assessment, *See also* Electronic portfolios (ePortfolios)
history of, 36
print portfolios, 78–86
in technotopic narratives of writing assessment, 35–37
Position statements, on predictions, 47–52
Positivism, 75
Poststructuralism, 79
Prediction, 46–52
and evolution of writing assessment technologies, 46–47, 128–133
of future needs of writing instruction, 48–52
key questions, 46
magnitude of missed projections, 47
new assessment technologies and, 46–52
position statements, 47–52
prediction bias, 40
predictive nature of writing assessments, 40

Prediction bias, 40
Predictive validity, 40
Prensky, Marc, 28
Prezi, 76
Print portfolios
    electronic portfolios versus, 79–81
    evolution of electronic portfolios from,
        78–86
Professional development, assessment
    process in, 2
Psychometric assessment, 61
Purdue University, 124
Putt, Archibald, 42

Quality enhancement plans (QEPs), 30–31

Racial discrimination, 23, 38–39, 40
Rademacher, C., 10
Reading-comprehension tests, 118
Reflective process, 38, 86–91
    examples of student reflections, 87–88
    as point of assessment for teachers of
        writing, 88–89
    sample descriptors in scoring guides,
        89–90
    self-assessment in, 86–89
    value of student reflections, 98
Reliability of assessments
    cost-effectiveness and, 63
    interrater, 115–117
    thermometer analogy for, 114–115
    validity versus, 110–111, 114–117
Responsibility model, as alternative to
    accountability measures, 30
Reynolds, N., 89
Rhetorical principles in text, 24, 67, 69, 71,
    74, 77, 78–79, 94–95, 99–100
Rice, Jeff, 11
Rife, M. C., 2
Ross, D., 27
Rossen-Knill, D. F., 28
Royer, D. J., 28
Rubrics, grading, 10, 62–63, 83, 95–96,
    113

Sagan, Carl, 15
Saturday Night Fever (movie), 34–35
SAT Verbal exam
    active adoption, 25
    bias in, 23, 38–39, 40
    direct assessment and, 61

efficiency of, 37
innovation and, 50–51
summer writing assessment and, 119
Writing portion, 22, 29, 37, 38–39, 43, 49,
    130
Scharton, M., 114
Schendel, E., 28, 53
Selber, S. A., 2, 77
Self-assessment, 86–89
Selfe, Cynthia, 1–2, 11, 21, 31, 45–46, 56, 98,
    106
Shallis, M., 25
Shaw, E. J., 38–39
Shepard, Lorie, 40, 110, 119
Sheppard, Jennifer, 11
SMART Boards, 56
Smith, J. B., 87
Smith, William L., 61, 63–64, 85, 117
Social bookmarking, 76, 93
Social networking, 16, 76, 93, 107–108
Sommers, J., 28, 35, 79
Sorapure, Madeleine, 95
Spellings Commission, 7
Sponsorship, of new technologies, 54–55
Springsteen, Bruce, 102–103
Standardized assessment, 22–23
Stroupe, Craig, 11, 48, 77–79, 103
Sturken, M., 33
Sudol, R., 27
Summative assessment, 55
Swimming metaphor, for writing
    assessment as technology, 6–7
Szymanski, Natalie, 35

Takayoski, P., 7
Tassoni, J. P., 28
Taylor, Todd W., 120–121, 123
Teaching Writing as Reflective Practice
    (Hillocks), 38
Tech envy, 16
Technicism, 34–35
Technological imperative, 24–25
Technological invisibility, determinism and,
    17, 23–27, 29–30
Technological narratives, 31–32
Technological neutrality, 17, 18–23
Technological sociology, 15
Technologies
    defining, 18
    function within society, 18–19
    physical nature of, 18

writing assessment as, *See* Writing assessment as technology

writing assessment with, *See* Writing assessment with technology

Technology and Literacy (Selfe), 31

Technophilia, 38

Technophobia, 37–41

  grand claims of new technologies and, 38–39

  technophilia versus, 38

  unintended consequences of new technologies and, 37–38, 55–56, 118–120

Technotopic narratives of writing assessments, 34–37

  antidominant view of technology (Barton), 35–36

  core beliefs, 34

  critical theory, 35–36

  efficiency, 36–37, 75

  need for new technologies, 36–37

  portfolio assessments, 35–37

  technicism, 34–35

Terministic screens (Burke), 45

Term wars, writing versus composing, 92–93

Test bias

  content bias, 39

  label bias, 39

  methodological bias, 39–40

  prediction bias, 40

  racial and gendered discrimination, 23, 38–39, 40, 119

Texting, 78

Text messages, 56

Theory hope (Fish), 34–35

Thomas, D., 33

Timed writing tests, 22, 36, 37, 38–39, 43, 49

Transparency of writing assessments as technologies, 27–31

  commonality and, 27–29

  determinism and, 27

  institutional acceptance and, 27–28, 29–30

  instrumentalism and, 27

  more pressing concerns and, 28, 30–31

Turkle, Sherry, 23–24, 40

Tweeting, 78

Twitter, 76, 108

Unified construct validity, 112–120

  appropriateness and accuracy of decisions, 113–114, 117–120

in framework to assess writing and assessment technologies, 112–114

old frameworks for new assessments, 126–127

Unintended consequences, of new assessment technologies, 37–38, 55–56, 118–120

University of North Carolina, Chapel Hill, 123

Validity of assessment, validity, as term, 114

Validity of assessments

  appropriateness and, 117–120

  as argument measured by degree, 113–117

  construct validity, 109–120, 126–127, 130

  content validity, 110

  criterion-related validity, 110

  debates concerning, 111

  defining, 109

  predictive validity, 40

  reliability versus, 110–111, 114–117

  in traditional framework of assessment, 112–113

Vantage for the College Board, 68–69

Vantage Technologies, 68

VHS platform, 51

Viagra, 49

Vie, S., 2

Vocabulary tests, 118

Volti, R., 6

Vuvox, 76

Wajcman, Joy, 8

Web publishing, 101

Web sites, 93

Westrum, Ron, 6–7, 23, 46

What We Really Value (Broad), 62–63, 85

White, Ed M., 40, 63, 109

Whitehead, Alfred North, 1

Whithaus, Carl, 65

Wiggins, G. P., 61

Wikis, 16, 56, 76, 93, 108

Williamson, M. M., 30, 36–37, 61

Winner, Langdon, 15, 21, 34, 38

Wohlpart, A. J., 10

Wordle, 76

Word processing, 27, 65–66, 93

Wright, Frank Lloyd, 59

WritePlacer Plus, 68–69, 71

Writing, composing versus, 92–93

Writing assessment as technology, 6–9, 15–56
  assumptions underlying, 8–9, 15–32
  basic assessment technology, 8
  course goals and, 3–4
  cultural narratives in, 33–41
  cultural understanding and, 6–7
  new assessment technologies, 42–56
  (re)evolution of writing and its
    assessment, 46–47, 128–133
  student outcomes and, 3–4
  swimmer metaphor for, 6–7
  teacher knowledge of technology, 2
  technotopic narratives of, 34–37
  types of assessments, 3, 36, 41
  values underlying assessments, 7–8
  writing assessment with technology
    versus, 5
Writing assessment with technology, 6,
  9–12, 59–127
  assessment issues with hyperactive
    hypertechs, 86–91, 96–99, 103–104,
    106–127
  authentic text and, 72
  authentic writing contexts in, 12, 128–129
  changing nature of writing and
    assessment technologies, 11, 106–127
  connections between course outcomes
    and specific technologies, 109,
    120–126, 127
  digital texts and technologies, 10–12,
    76–127
  electronic portfolios (ePortfolios), 5, 10–11,
    35–37, 43–44, 50–52, 55, 60, 79, 81–86

grading rubrics, 10, 62–63, 83, 95–96,
  113
holistic scoring, 10, 17, 29, 36, 63–65,
  95–96
mechanization process, 9–10, 59–75
(re)evolution of writing and its
  assessment, 46–47, 128–133
writing assessment as technology versus,
  5
Writing experts
  as basis for assessment, 117
  framing the assessment problem, 54–55
  machine-scored student writing and,
    70–74
  role in developing new assessment
    technologies, 41, 43, 53–55, 70–74
  writing outcomes, 120–126, 127
  Writing Program Administrators (WPA),
    40, 43, 120–126
Writing New Media (Selfe), 98
Writing Program Administrators (WPA), 40,
  43, 120–126
  considering implementation of
    hypertech, 121–126
  integrating technologies into composition
    classes, 120–126
  obstacles to implementing technology,
    123–126
  Outcomes Statement, 121–122
Wysocki, Anne F., 92, 94

Yancey, K. B., 46, 77, 79–82, 87
YouTube, 76

About the Author

MICHAEL NEAL is an assistant professor in the English department at Florida State University, where he explores intersections between composition, writing assessments, multimodal literacies, and technologies in his research and teaching. He received his PhD from the University of Louisville, his MA from Ball State University, and a BA in English from Taylor University. Neal has taught undergraduate courses in 1st-year composition, technical writing, advanced article and essay writing, and visual rhetoric; he also has taught graduate courses in composition theory, research methods, visual rhetoric, and teacher preparation courses. Neal has directed 1st-year composition, served as an ePortfolio faculty fellow, and delivered workshops and consultations on writing across the curriculum and electronic portfolio initiatives.